Beneath the Matterhorn

Odd Revelations and Sober
Observations by an Airbnb Host in
Zermatt, Switzerland

Mark Inglin

DEDICATION

To my son Erich, wherever he may be.

mountain behind
mama's house
Zermatt, Switzerland

Contents

ACKNOWLEDGMENTS

I thank my creative editor, Melanie Saxton, for inspiration and content contribution that allowed this manuscript to evolve beyond the uni-dimensional. Peter Blanchard generously contributed his time to help me find those hidden errors. Deep appreciation goes to Manhui Jin for providing the cover art, and to Vladimir Stojanovic for the cover design. And even down in Milan, Ke Song—violinist and emoji queen—had me see beyond the horizon.

ii.

Preface

The motivation for writing this book arose from two sources. First, I wished to inform readers about life as an Airbnb host in a renowned Swiss village, bustling with tourists and featuring one of the world's premier natural attractions—the majestic Matterhorn. For those who may not know, Airbnb is an online marketplace that matches guests seeking to share accommodations with hosts at a price. In my case as host, I welcome a cross section of adventurers who have made Zermatt their destination.

The second reason for writing this book relates to a personal history far removed from the lightheartedness and joy associated with the first; both motivations meet by fate and go hand in hand in this village.

The personal history revealed here has relevance beyond this secluded valley of the Matterhorn and is based on topics in two previous books. Yes, I have had to keep a secret, literally to survive. The storytelling path allows me to share not only an eagle's view of Zermatt, but also a notorious and unlikely history kept necessarily, strategically and successfully from nearly six hundred guests during four years as a host in Zermatt— the last two as a Superhost. In revealing that history I share the lessons learned in exploring what is seen as true, the sources of what we believe to be true, and why stereotypes and generalizations have fundamental appeal.

Why is maintaining an open mind in the face of our assumptions so difficult? Is what we conclude to be rational based adequately on truth, or are we hoodwinked into false conclusions?

The battle fought between fact and the fiction that disguises as such is waged with stories that we tell and hear, and it affects what we buy, where we vacation, and who we vote for—and, in general, what we should *believe*.

"All I know is just what I read in the papers, and that's an alibi for my ignorance," Will Rogers quipped. While news that is fake isn't new, what *is* new is how effective, widespread and rapidly life altering it has become.

By unlikely fate, the Matterhorn of Zermatt has become a muse for me, while residence in Switzerland affords me the luxury of defying an American court order to stop writing about lawyer misconduct back home.

Wherever we go in the world, what isn't true about you, me, or anyone else can follow … even to the heart of a small, Swiss village. I should know, for I've lived it firsthand. I'm fortunate, however, to have the opportunity to disprove fake news in the most effective way I know how… living here in Zermatt and writing.

This little book is one more effort to fight back against strong forces intent on redefining reality, as the reader will discover.

The observations made and the views expressed in the chapters ahead are delivered from my personal perspective on Swiss culture—made whimsically, occasionally wittily and, I hope, wisely. I make no claim, however, to having done formal research on every facet of this book, other than living in Switzerland and observing carefully for fifteen years, four of those in Zermatt.

I share experiences and narratives relayed to me by others as an outsider hailing from the USA, but born in Switzerland to parents who had extensive Swiss roots. My command of the Swiss-German dialect is so close to native that locals may, at times, assume that I am "of the tribe," a relatively rare attribute for someone reared entirely outside of Switzerland. When needed, I can also deploy an American accent, which allows me to mingle forthrightly with tourists and foreigners who live and work in Switzerland. They reveal their feelings to me openly, as one foreigner to another. This hybrid status enables me to see Switzerland from both inside and out, and adds a unique duality to this book's perspective.

Through my efforts here, I hope to show why everyone has a story that needs to be heard but not told by others on their behalf. Here is my story of life in Zermatt, the strange way in which I came to live in Switzerland, and how I have learned to deal with fake news.

Author's note: To preserve anonymity, names and identifying features have been altered in the accounts that follow concerning events that took place during my hosting.

~ Mark Inglin
Zermatt, 2019

I.   A Secret at the Foot of the Matterhorn

"In an ideal world, I'd spend every weekend at my home in Zermatt in Switzerland." ~ Vanessa Mae, British violinist

Extraordinary circumstances sent an American back to the country of his birth—Switzerland— and later on to the renowned village of Zermatt. I am the American, and the "circumstances" involve the USA legal system and violations of First Amendment rights— profound and life-altering indeed. You might now wonder what these violations have to do with a book about tourists, the Matterhorn, and the Swiss in general. Well, in a convoluted series of twists and turns, my fate in the USA motivated me to cross the Atlantic—an escape in the true sense of the word— seeking refuge in the arms of the Swiss and ultimately becoming an Airbnb host.

As will occasionally happen in life, people, places and events in this story merged in unanticipated ways. It was that mix of fate that I thought would make for interesting and informative reading.

I will expound on the chain of events that led me to Zermatt in a form that I hope is a bonus of sorts to readers: tourist information, yes, but with a touch of true crime that includes cross-continental intrigue.

The backstory begins in Milwaukee, Wisconsin, spans to Switzerland and includes an international fugitive. There may be quite a few books that raise a comparable theme in a generic way as a thriller, but not many that can be classified as non-fiction.

1

It would have been too farfetched for me to have foreseen my improbable trajectory to Zermatt— even as fiction it would have appeared contrived. In addition to returning to my ancestral roots out of legal necessity, I became an Airbnb host to guests from every corner of the world without any plan to do so. I am proud to state that I'm not just a host now, but one who has attained Superhost status for nine quarters in a row with a series of five-star ratings and closing-in on 600 guests.

Today I enjoy a satisfying life in an apartment overlooking the valley that leads directly to the base of the Matterhorn, with sparkle added by the personalities who enter my front door. I've managed to find considerable solace here in Zermatt as well; I am fortunate to call the town beneath the mountain of mountains "home" and at the same time have people from around the world visit and inspire me.

The neighbors downstairs once asked, "How can you just invite strangers into your home like that?" Well, the answer is easy: Those strangers—their stories, habits, quirks and emotions—add immensely to my enjoyment of day-to-day living in a relatively isolated Swiss village.

For four years now, hosting via Airbnb has been my pleasant window to the wider world in this mountain-cloistered but very frequently visited Swiss village. Guests experience my hospitality, receive destination tips, join me at mealtimes, and share their lives and stories. Sometimes, in the relative sanctum of my home, they entrust me with their deepest secrets. However, they all remain unaware that I keep a secret of my own … well, at least until now.

Guests, of course, are equally interested in me and their curiosity often includes the question, "What motivated you to host outsiders in your apartment?"

"Well, it's simple," I explain. "I just felt lonely." And that is how my hosting career began.

***

Why Zermatt? I moved here after living in the town of Interlaken for eleven years, not far from the Swiss capitol, Berne. Interlaken is also a village widely known as a tourist destination of even higher rank than Zermatt in terms of numbers of foreign visitors. The owner of the house that I lived in—a close friend—died unexpectedly. I was forced to move when her children sold the place.

I wasn't particularly sorry about leaving Interlaken. With a disruptive influx of Chinese money buying up the shops and more tourists than were appreciated, the locals weren't keen on outsiders in their social mix. After living there for eleven years I still felt like a stranger.

I have traveled extensively throughout Switzerland and am aware of the astonishing beauty of so many places in this small country. I've always been attracted to the area known as the Valais, the home canton of Zermatt nestled on the border of Switzerland with Italy, more so than anywhere else. The mythology attached to the Valais is as interesting as the iconic shape of the Matterhorn itself, with its faces chiseled in four directions, the north and east being the most prominent and readily identifiable.

Legend has it that a giant named Gargantua and his accomplice, Cervin, used to stomp across the landscape of the Valais. Gargantua inadvertently dropped a bag of earth, creating the hill upon which the Valais sits. Cervin's footsteps caused surrounding ridges and mountains to collapse, leaving only a triangular shape between his legs—the Matterhorn.

3

Matterhorn, the German name, blends the words matte, meaning "meadow," and horn, meaning "peak." *Mont Cervin* is French for Matterhorn (*Monte Cervino* in Italian)—and both words derive from the Latin *Cervus*, a genus of deer and elk. However you spell it, this iconic tourist attraction is one of the most photographed landmarks in Switzerland, rising 4,478 m (14,691 ft.).

Perhaps you've seen a more diminutive model of our mountain in Disneyland. Walt Disney himself visited the Matterhorn in the 1950s and was inspired to build a miniature version—a bobsledding rollercoaster involving a snow-capped mountain, a speeding sled, and the Abominable Snowman.

Recently, the Swiss have become "picky" about others using the Matterhorn in their branding. You may have seen the Matterhorn on bottles of Old Spice deodorant and on triangular boxes of well-known Toblerone chocolate, which harbors the camouflaged shape of a bear depicted inside the mountain—a fact that few note. But as for newer marketing ploys, there has been a crackdown. It is less likely that the image of the Matterhorn will be exploited for commercial gain … except as a delightful draw for tourists.

Those of us here in Zermatt depend mightily on our tourists, who flock to this haven of beauty and nature to escape concrete jungles elsewhere. Foreign visitors are not only my personal window to the world, but they have also sculpted this village and, indeed, much of Switzerland.

This country leaves strong impressions of cleanliness, efficiency, reliability and rectitude to go along with the overwhelming beauty. Live here longer, however, and a quick realization will settle in: the Swiss are also human.

II. The Thing About the Swiss ...

"Everything that irritates us about others can lead us to an understanding of ourselves."
~ Carl Jung, Swiss psychologist and psychiatrist

It was more than just the Matterhorn that drew me to Zermatt. I was attracted to the area by below average humidity and the appeal of less rainfall, which translates to more sunshine. The mountainsides in many places appear sparser of vegetation, with fewer dark conifers that predominate in other areas to the very tops of mountains that are often lower. This relative absence of darkness higher up provides a wilder, lonelier, more expansive look afar.

Zermatt itself is surrounded by rare deciduous conifers known as larch trees. From a distance they may appear as ordinary mountain pines, but they turn an appealing rusty-orange color in the fall and lose their needle-leaves entirely for the winter. This provides pleasant fall coloring, a sign of seasonal change that is not as intense elsewhere in the country.

Valleys near Zermatt in this canton appear broader, flatter and have more exposed, lighter-colored rock. This lightness and the relative openness lead to less of a brooding feel. Tall, straight poplar trees, also a feature less common elsewhere, pleasantly interrupt views in the valleys here and there. Drenched in the many days of sunshine, these valleys epitomize the peaceful and the tranquil.

Or, I might have chosen Zermatt for what I consider a more relaxed attitude by the locals—friendlier in many ways, with conversations less strained and including more smiles. I cannot pinpoint exactly why that should be the case. Perhaps it's due to the large percentage of foreigners who live and work in the area. They certainly influence the locals with their more sociable manners, unlike the often-dour, keep-your-distance Swiss, who are quite restrictive with their emotions and personal invitations.

While the town of Interlaken also hosts tourists who represent the most varied cultures, dress and habits, for my taste it retains a noticeable lack of hospitality, offering fewer signs of a genuine welcome to tourists. That is not my experience here in Zermatt, even though we are more isolated geographically and off the beaten path. Arrival is to a formidable, mountainous cul-de-sac after a relatively long train ride through a narrow valley.

I claim that here in Zermatt the happiness expressed by our abundant tourists at seeing our hostess, Lady Matterhorn, mellows some of the Swiss rigidity. All combined, this is a special place; I feel more at home in Zermatt than anywhere else in Switzerland.

***

A few words need to be said about the Swiss as a whole before I proceed. This information further explains my reason for hosting strangers from afar in Zermatt.

A caveat, though, before I launch into my mostly but not entirely personal perceptions of the Swiss. Here and throughout this book I single out the Swiss for particular traits and do so against the backdrop of my own Swiss ancestry. With this awareness, I keep in mind that environments mold any culture and, in turn, the individuals who live there. The Swiss are not the descendants of cold-blooded aliens, as some outsiders claim. The environment that sculpted the Swiss character is simply not that of Tahiti.

The Swiss do as they do for reasons—some good and some not so—even while those reasons are not readily evident or understandable. The outsider to the country is obviously a keen observer, as he/she has two vantage points from which to judge. The existence of two perspectives results in the desire to compare, to describe, to formulate opinions and to criticize.

Like most perfectionists, the Swiss do not always take kindly to criticism. Foreigners here, many of whom come from countries less advantaged, tend to keep their complaints within their own, trusted circles. The Swiss themselves, however, will routinely offer criticism after visiting a foreign land, in the form of pronouncing shortcomings compared to the way things are done (properly, competently) back home in the jewel of Europe. It may not be the duty of the privileged to point out the faults and frailties of others of lessor circumstances, but it does seem to be a habit.

While the Swiss can be said to be many good things, including on the whole industrious, practical, thrifty, law-abiding, clean, neat, orderly, technically competent, serious-minded, outstanding in their care of the elderly and the disabled, generally reliable and certainly formally polite initially ... they will never be accused of being overly sociable or easy with hospitality, of sharing their emotions or admitting to fault. They are, on the whole, simply not outgoing or spontaneous souls—at least not so with an outsider. Overly suspicious, mistrustful and cautious, with a tendency toward what looks like deceit due to an aversion to confrontation, is how many from the outside see the Swiss. This impression is not without its foundation.

An Italian scientist acquaintance curses the Swiss vehemently for what he calls their sense of cultural superiority, he having been denied housing based on his ethnicity. There are still Swiss of a certain mindset who feel that Italians are, and should remain, exceptionally well suited to road construction.

This friend jokes that the Swiss lack a "social gene." There are plenty of ex-pats living in Switzerland who feel the same way, never mind asking the folks of non-European ethnicity or dark skin color how they feel about the native inhabitants of the country.

We can't all be the inviting "Swiss Miss" featured in the 1960s on boxes of cocoa. Today, the iconic blonde maiden no longer appears in the branding, but her influence lives on as an image evoked by the name alone. A dollop of trivia here: circa 1963, fans of that brand could send three dollars and a box top to the company in return for a "genuine Swiss Miss doll."

Then again, the most touching acts of genuine, caring community concern are also evident in Switzerland. A generosity of spirit is much evident in the treatment of, for example, the less mentally fortunate. Bus trips to museums or to the zoo are arranged, and dinner outings are organized for people who might be living on the streets in the USA, or simply recognized as failures and dismissed. Here, the elderly and the unfortunate are not forgotten. This effort truly succeeds in making sure that people do not drop too far to the bottom of the social heap. We do not see homeless people here. I admire the Swiss a great deal for such inclusiveness and generosity. It's a capitalist country, but there is still some heart that noticeably remains.

Publicly funded care centers for the elderly are often located in the best parts of town, with up-to-date features and care apparently not spared. The most modern, well thought out facilities exist to put the psychologically frail to work on useful crafts and such, so that they, too, are contributing members—all planned for the benefit of the overall community. Cemeteries are cared for meticulously, including fresh flowers. It is a collectively agreed-upon generosity, however, that seems strangely thwarted as soon as justice for the individual implies the threat of change or disruption to settled hierarchy. The apparent generosity exemplifies a tolerance that is not shown at what we can call the other end of the spectrum. Woe to the rebel or misfit who challenges the system from strength. The culture seems to whole-heartedly agree with Rudyard Kipling's poem, *If*: "And yet don't look too good, nor talk too wise."

What so many foreigners living in Switzerland perceive as arrogance or an air of superiority among the Swiss, however, is merely a surface coating, an inferiority complex in disguise. Take this example, the famous encounter between Oprah Winfrey and a salesperson in a fashion store on the Bahnhofstrasse of Zurich, a shopping area known for it high prices. Winfrey asked the clerk, who had no idea who she is, if she might see a particular handbag on a shelf, for inspection. The clerk, trying to be helpful as it were, politely informed Winfrey that the bag would be too expensive for her! "Can I show you something more affordable?" (i.e. Italians are good for road construction, and black people are poor.) Oprah, it was reported, was not amused.

In this case, ignorance and stereotyping were the villains. But the substrate to such perceived arrogance is often a defense mechanism, the assemblage of a lack of wider experience and self-confidence and insecurity derived from feeling too small and powerless, yet coupled with being an obviously attractive country and enjoying out-sized financial success.

While not recognizing ones vulnerabilities can lead to arrogance, an awareness of those same vulnerabilities that is too keen can lead to what may be incorrectly interpreted as arrogance.

III.   A National Mindset

"Switzerland would be a mighty big place if it were ironed flat."
~ Mark Twain, American writer and humorist

The history of Switzerland is embossed with its geography, a nation assembled of small villages and narrow valleys in which farming was difficult, tradition ran deep, and there was no escape to California if things went south. One canton alone, Graubünden, lays claim to one hundred and fifty valleys and associated small villages.

It is well known that valleys isolated by physical barriers can give rise to distinct species of plants and animals. It's readily intuitive that cultures can also distinguish themselves among islands of small villages roosted in narrow valleys. The geographic isolation of the past fostered psychological isolation in these valleys. Distinct strategies therefore emerged on how to survive, ranging from legitimate to dubious practices.

What kind of dubious practices set isolated pockets of thought apart? For example, as late as 2013 the Swiss lower house of parliament voted to raise the legal age of prostitution from sixteen to eighteen, a minor victory for idealism (aided by a push from the European Union) against the pragmatism that sways much of Swiss thinking.

This tidbit of information may be irrelevant to an average tourist, but it sheds light on how outside influences can remain alien locally in Switzerland, just as the Canton of Appenzell refrained from permitting women the right to vote until, astonishingly, 1990.

Change and criticism from the outside aimed at tight village pockets are not suffered gladly, again in the midst of an atmosphere of relatively outstanding financial success, as Switzerland enjoys. Not much need to second-guess yourself if your paycheck is fatter than most. After all, is financial success not universally applauded as evidence of superiority?

We are small, insignificant, powerless here ... yet relatively wealthy. Anyway, that is the perception of Switzerland from the outside. Fault acknowledgement under such circumstances is not a characteristic of a culture of smallness and insignificance, certainly not when the average bank account is reported as 50,000 Swiss francs!

A conceit has crept in here and there, that prosperity is due to working harder and being special (perhaps superior) relative to the outsider, and less so to possible fortune derived from convenient circumstances or geographic fate at the center of Europe. The luxury of being able to sidestep major world problems or responsibilities by considering oneself conveniently inconsequential ... has been a Swiss tradition.

Just as the Matterhorn is a predominant visual symbol of Switzerland, neutrality is the characterizing ideology associated with the nation. It is the political hallmark of Switzerland. The Swiss reach for the word as defense against this or that line of inconvenient reasoning. It is both a stance and a reaction, past and present.

In 2018 National Public Radio (NPR) reported the following quote from its popular radio show *Wait, Wait, Don't Tell Me*. It reflected a common perception:

"It's tough to get the Swiss to take a side. Even the Nazi's couldn't do it."

The quote, however, was followed by the story of a woman who was denied Swiss citizenship in a small village because she was an annoying vegan and an animal rights activist who wished to see the end of ringing church- and cow bells. Neutrality regarding her unwelcome attitudes was rapidly cast aside. She was invited to go elsewhere.

The Swiss indeed will not hesitate in taking a tough stance, but if the Swiss eye sees issues in the world beyond the national borders associated with a cost, then neutrality may conveniently kick-in. For some, neutrality is just cheap salve, another word for not knowing what to stand for or being too aware that taking a stand will have economic consequences.

Neutrality has its psychological roots in Switzerland's size and position among neighbors who were historically more culturally advanced, powerful and influential. If your big brothers are fighting and you have no choice but to remain in the house, being neutral is a not a bad survival strategy.

I'll share my favorite, infamous example of how the Swiss reach for the overused, misused concept of neutrality as deflection, as an excuse for the commission of sins or the omission of responsibility. The 1988 Lockerbie bombing, in which Pan Am flight 103 was blasted from the sky by Libyan terrorists, is the incident that I cite. The timing device for the bomb, it was shown, traced back to a sale by a Swiss electronics firm in Zurich. Should the company have been aware that something was afoul by the specifications submitted for the order: high-altitude triggering?

In defense, it was reported that the owner of the

company made reference to Swiss neutrality. This did not need to make any actual sense. Neutrality is a magical word; it was used speciously as a diplomatic sidestep to the issue of morality and responsibility for, here, a crime.

The more powerless one feels, and the closer one feels to the edge of survival, the greater the justification for selfish acts perhaps not considered (not dared to be considered) unacceptable in Switzerland, but everywhere else. The core Swiss insecurity has not been extinguished by the nation's financial success.

While the nation claims political neutrality, at the same time the Swiss military has nevertheless gained a worldwide favorable reputation. The Swiss do not meddle in the affairs of other countries, but they do participate in international peacekeeping missions and the army has amassed a sort of cult following, at least commercially. The military here has also deeply influenced the Swiss culture.

Military activity in the form of mercenaries and regional soldiers has extensive roots in Switzerland, as Swiss troops went to war quite often in the Late Middle Ages. Readers may be familiar with the role of Swiss soldiers today in the Pontifical Swiss Guard, the Pope's army. These bodyguards to the Pope are among the oldest military units in continuous operation (established in 1506 under Pope Julius II). Recruits must be Swiss Catholic males between 19 and 30 years of age who have completed basic training with the Swiss Armed Forces, and they must be unmarried. This requirement, surely, is a part of Catholic tradition that has proven itself less than morally successful to date: "One American cardinal has been banned from the Vatican and sent back to the United States for his improper conduct with a Swiss Guard," writes French investigative journalist Frédéric

Martel.

Speaking to one of the guards, Martel hears vented in dismay that, "The harassment is so insistent that I said to myself that I was going straight home. Many of us are exasperated by the usually rather indiscreet advances of the cardinals and bishops."

Wow! Not exactly an optimal recruiting message for papal guards!

As is readily evident from souvenir shop offerings and purchases ranging from knives to canteens and backpacks that bear a Swiss Military inscription, the entire world seems to be aware of and enthralled by the Swiss military. Take the Swiss Army knife, for example. In the late 1880s, the Swiss devised folding pocketknives (with a screwdriver) for their soldiers. This allowed opening cans and the disassembly and reassembly of rifles. The knife is a cultural phenomenon much admired around the world and seen, for example, on the U.S. TV show *McGyver*, not to mention deployment into space by NASA since the 1970s. Its various models are still used and collected around the globe.

Today, Switzerland's civilian population constitutes its army to a large degree. There are 21,000 active army personnel, but 120,000 reservists. Unless granted a civil service function, more or less every male of age eighteen and above is required to serve in the military for eleven years, training in the army a number of weeks annually and regularly. Dispensation from employer requirements is mandatory for this service, in some cases until age thirty seven. Swiss soldiers have traditionally been permitted to take their equipment and weapons home after their basic training. A weapon then belongs to them for life. Small Switzerland thus effectively winds up with one of the largest armies in the world.

Serving in the Swiss military also means that each soldier discovers the lay of their culturally diverse land and interacts with fellow soldiers from other cantons, perhaps regions speaking another language. This builds strong friendships and a national cohesion. At the same time, a large portion of the male population has been influenced by regimentation and respect for authority in that way. Inculcated in youth and with regular reminders, the lessons of just following orders and thus staying out of trouble can begin to stick, subtly influencing interactions in civilian life.

With the easing of tensions with the Soviet Union, or Russia, after the fall of the Berlin Wall, questions were raised by the Swiss as to the worth of their military in any practical sense. Today, many young men can choose to serve their country in a civilian capacity, for example in a hospital or nursing home in place of the army. Also, not every man is permitted to take his weapon home these days, depending on their past, personal history and psychological test results. Those who do take home a weapon have restricted access to ammunition.

The overall situation with weapons ownership in general for the Swiss public is also somewhat more restrictive today. Application must be made with the police. Background checks are mandatory and the right of refusal is exercised. Automatic weapons are illegal and semi-automatic weapons are restricted. There is no weapons store in Zermatt. Buying a hunting rifle, for example, requires a trip to a larger town a few hours away. At least so far, Switzerland does not have an exhibitionist-style gun culture. Among Swiss men, swagger and machismo also express themselves in more reserved fashion in most regards compared to the American stereotype, as one would expect from the reserved nature of the culture. On the other hand, the #MeToo movement may not be as robust as in the States. Male dominance is still largely taken for granted here, at least as determined by the local attitudes that I witness. Consider this published gem by a Zermatt tourism director, referring to our lovely Lady Matterhorn: "I see it every morning and evening in a different light. Even with clouds it changes its face. It's like having a different wife every day in front of your door."

Mocking the USA's #MeToo movement, an attitude that serves as an excellent defense mechanism, a local Swiss male friend wondered how the Americans intended to have babies in the future, i.e. if males cannot be dominant, what could be left for them to do?

This is not a country with the manifestation of personal power or boasting among its traditions. There is certainly boasting, but it is often done at the local community or national level in the form of collective pride, for example evident from the abundant number of Swiss and local flags flying or the obvious pride in the continuing references to Swiss quality.

Communities demonstrate local pride through their specific activity groups, for example musical bands, associations that maintain traditional costumes, groups specializing in local history, etc. Patriotism in Switzerland is every bit as fervent as in the USA, but more tradition-related and evident at the local level, and fostered by the understanding that things are materially quite good here.

Not long ago, I had an encounter with a guest in my home who broke the mold entirely by displaying machismo and obvious remnants of Swiss military influence together with unbridled ego. It was, without doubt, the strangest experience I had had —let's just call it bizarre—three years into my hosting career. This Swiss guest, a man of about fifty years of age, was angry even before he arrived. From the start of his visit, he objected to the fact that I had published house rules for the location, for example a latest arrival time of 7 p.m. (which he violated by three and a half hours).

One of his first remarks was, "Why do you have so many rules?"

This observation took me aback. I didn't think I had too many rules, and no one had ever complained.

"Your house rules," he continued, "remind me of the military."

Strange, I thought. It's not like he's forced to stay with me.

I explained to my guest that house rules are stipulated clearly in advance to help me avoid, for example, having obnoxious guests who wish to return from pubs in the early morning hours. And published rules allow potential guests to know what to expect, thereby permitting them to book some other location.

In response, there and then he bolted from the sofa and fumed, "But you run this place like a military camp. It's just like being in the military!"

This shock not being adequate, he then marched outside, onto the guest balcony, shouting same for all of the neighbors to hear!

As this had not been his first reference to the military, it dawned on me that he obviously had some deep, emotional connection with that organization. Needless to say, I was encouraged to suggest that we end his self-imposed imprisonment in my camp as soon as possible. I informed him that I play by the statistics. At that time I had achieved Superhost status five times in a row with five-star ratings from guests—and I shared this information with my agitated visitor.

"Such stats are good enough for me," I explained.

Obviously, most people like staying in the home of General George S. Patton reincarnate.

What happened when he left should not have been a surprise; it was pure Swiss.

When in doubt about bad behavior in Switzerland, above all make sure things are … clean and orderly. The worst sin in Switzerland is not being … clean and orderly.

Some intriguing, related psychological research does indeed show that feelings of guilt and cleanliness are all entangled in the human mind, sort of like sex and the Catholic Church. The feeling of washing away guilt by literally washing one's hands is but one example. Feeling guilty? Time to scrub that floor and have it shine. Make an ass of yourself, okay. Act ugly and offensive to a host, that's fine. But for God's sake, make sure you leave the place in orderly shape, for that is the path to redemption.

Perhaps for anyone other than a Swiss, or anyone completely dissatisfied with my hosting as this man clearly was, I would have expected a departure with little concern for the organization of bedding. But my Swiss guest made his bed to exacting military specifications before he left. The used towel was placed on the pillow, perfectly folded. Bedding was left without a crease. The two longitudinal sides of the bedspread were both folded in toward the center, presumably as taught in the military.

Remarkably, my departing guest then took two photos of his creation, apparently to prove that the bedding was up to the highest standards upon departure. He was not going to let me accuse him of being a poor guest because he left behind anything but a bed perfect to the eye. I was amazed and amused. I wash all bedding after each guest departs anyway, and in no way would I have had him court-martialed for an untidy bed.

Of course, this is just one anecdote representing one guest on whom the military had made a deep impression, perhaps he was resentful of some failure to achieve rank—or who knows what. Alone he certainly was not, however, in regard to his memories of Swiss military service sometimes long in the past, as I have heard nostalgically repeated. But by and large, military memories as passed on to me have been positive, referring to times of great joy on army maneuvers in the mountains and to the deep friendships made.

Just recently, I encountered an old, former Swiss soldier who complained extensively about how today's Swiss military is too soft on recruits. Justification for the observation? They have put roller wheels on military luggage.

"In my day, we had to carry our luggage. What is the world coming to?"

I wonder what his reaction was after the Swiss military announced recently that soldiers could wear shorts and t-shirts instead of standard gear in a bout of excessively hot weather. Swiss high command, after all, did not expect the Russians to attack until the cold of winter.

***

For a seemingly mild-mannered country in so many other ways, there is nevertheless a deeper and darker streak of love of authority evident in Switzerland. *Folgsamkeit,* or obedience—often unquestioned—has outsized value here. This can also be referred to as "orderliness" or "the Swiss way."

Recently, a scam perpetrated on Swiss citizens involved fake police informing bank customers that they needed to withdraw money from their bank for some reason related to security, and they were then to allow the "police" to come to their home to retrieve it. The scam worked well enough, the explanation given being that "older" Swiss still respected authority to an unwarranted extent. I think the word "older" may have been mis-emphasized in this explanation.

A French guest once remarked that he observes Swiss along the border with France copying down the license plate numbers of people they see speeding, then they send the information to the Swiss police. The prohibition on being a "rat" is no match for the urge to follow rules (and making damn sure that everyone else follows them, too.)

In days past, anyone applying for Swiss citizenship was subject to home inspections, their living conditions scrutinized for the appropriate "orderliness." Dust on the shelves? Laundry strewn on the floor? Perhaps the applicant would feel more comfortable living in the San Fernando Valley area.

As I grew up with Swiss parents and was often exposed to the Swiss-German culture on visits back home and through Swiss family friends, little of the pedantic and the "We'll teach you" attitude on display here at times surprises me. (Note: my own parents were far more liberal.) But I am continually impressed by how effective this "orderliness" message and indoctrination is, and how the perception of Swiss technical and financial prowess on the part of newcomers to the country changes newcomer attitudes.

Switzerland is orderly, safe, stable, and economically successful; this culture and its ways must therefore appear superior to any outsider, especially those from poorer countries. These folks often quickly accept that they must change their easy-going ways and be perfectionist rule-followers, like the locals. They become staunch defenders of "orderliness" as demanded and defined by the culture; they wave the Swiss flag proudly.

There is a common expectation here that the voice of authority must equal righteousness. This is not a culture that breeds rebels. I have personally seen this authoritarianism evolve in two stages: shouting and anger and outright intimidation will be tried out at first against someone to stop any unpleasant activity, with threats of dire consequences for failure to obey an obvious rule of conduct. But then, if there is resistance and no sign of retreat, neutrality will suddenly kick-in and take over the agenda.

Let's be reasonable now. As a Swiss, you cannot continue to fight after your bluff has been called. You need to negotiate. Everything is seen as negotiable territory here, and that includes ideals or, at times, even the truth. When you are small, you cannot afford certain noble luxuries.

There is a story, as reported in the *New York Times* at the time of its happening, that merges well here and it goes as follows: At the early stages, when American lawyers first approached Swiss banks to repatriate money still held by those banks from the Holocaust and WWII, Swiss management intentionally kept the lawyers waiting for hours past the appointment time.

This type of defiance of the outsider strikes me as absolutely typical. Of course, no shouting or threats here—too public an issue—but a display of stubbornness. Why? Perhaps a primal response. Maybe they (or it) will go away? This doesn't have to make any logical sense. It certainly irritated the lawyers, who kept checking their Swiss watches. It was reported that this rude behavior set the lawyers on a more combative path of their own defiance and, of course, in the end they won.

From my experiences, I claim that this type of, in effect, shunning or denial when confronting threat or something unpleasant is psychologically engrained in the Swiss culture. It is a Swiss twist on a maxim by Joseph Stalin: If you stick your bayonet into someone and you encounter mush, keep pushing; if you encounter steel, stop.

Material survival is ever and always on the minds of the Swiss, who have been instructed from early on to realize that they are small, have no power in the world, and are not blessed with natural resources. This is a refrain often heard: no natural resources here. I counter by saying that natural beauty is a significant natural resource. Not for export, of course, but even better—it imports its own customers.

The answer the Swiss have given to the demands of survival without resources (tourism has not always been as significant and rewarding as it is today) is work hard, cohesion, and a conservative suspicion of change. Being small, we can't always afford the luxury of idealism or entertaining contrarian philosophies.

In my experience, limited as that may be, my impression is that Swiss men have mastered a full understanding of what it means to be physically courageous. There are plenty of solid role models and examples of physical courage to be found here, and that type of courage has becomes part of lore. Indeed, one might expect this from life amidst the dangers that mountains and mountaineering can pose. But physical courage and psychological courage are to different animals. It has also been my experience that many Swiss men will shrink and slink away from any overt challenge to tradition or hierarchy or to the status quo, regardless of any higher, worthy principle that might be argued. A drifting back to childhood and readily obeying the master's voice (or the army officer's voice) in tough psychological circumstances does not surprise me here, even if that leads to betrayal. Idealism is indeed the slave to the ever-dominant Swiss practicality.

It is impossible to grow up in this country and not think that you, too, are small. Combined with the referenced lack of natural resources, when any people think that all they have is small, then small becomes an excuse. The outsized, defensive reactions by the Swiss may well come as compensation for feeling that they have little influence in the world, due also to the country's lack of significant history. This explains why the preservation of a good image can surprisingly triumph over both truth and justice here, even in the legal system. It's that "clean image" that we desperately need to maintain.

Negotiation and quiet transactions between people per force have been the means of successful survival. While restraint and flying under the radar have certainly served the country well as a whole, this also minimizes the potential evolution of the rebel who may have ideas counter to the prevailing culture.

Not a few trailblazers in Switzerland decided to leave an atmosphere too restrictive for their future development once fame had been attained. Elisabeth Kübler-Ross, a Swiss-American psychiatrist and pioneer in near-death studies, comes readily to mind, as she railed against the restriction of a small country. (In her autobiography *Das Rad des Leben*s (*The Wheel of Life*) Kübler-Ross also mentions experiencing spiritual growth in Zermatt, but apparently not enough of it to have had her stay.)

Proof of this "we are insignificant" stance is shown by a recent report in the *Washington Post*. People from countries throughout the world were asked to rank the importance of their nation in world history. Russia ranked first in its claim to historical significance, the USA somewhere in the middle, but the Swiss themselves ranked Switzerland dead last.

Awkwardly stated, Switzerland doesn't have much history to celebrate, at least not in the conventional sense of dominance, conquest of landmasses by armies or bloody wars that put other countries on the map. The country's population, after all, is too small.

Russians, of course, enjoy great awareness of their cultural achievements in music and literature, and they are mightily proud of their still relatively vivid memories of their primary role as victors during the German scourge of WWII. The Swiss lack a sense of themselves in these regards, and it shows. Hefty bank accounts cannot compensate for such absences in history. It is always more difficult being forced to refer to "they" instead of "we" in such matters of potential national pride. And if you live in a land that would readily be called ideal by so many less fortunate souls from different geographical parts, the question arises, have the ideals that now prevail been established and defended locally or were they imported cheaply after being implemented by out-of-towners?

***

Something indicative that circles back to the concept of "tiny" emerges from the dialect of Swiss-German itself. It reflects the small, as the language frequently reverts to the diminutive form, with nouns gaining a "li" ending. This addition of "li" to the end of a word makes any noun smaller, reduces it down to bite-sized morsels, as if everything should shrink in order to remain manageable and controlled and in proportion to the size of the country. Example: cabinet: in German *Kasten,* Swiss-German *Kästli* (cabinet, cut down to size); parlor: in German *Stuben,* Swiss-German *Stübli,* and so on. It is, in fact, a verbal form of submission.

Some time ago, I met a journalist from Switzerland's largest newspaper. He was covering a scandal involving misadministration at a Swiss university. Mulling over how he should couch his final story for publication, and concerned about the negative reverberations for people whom he knew personally, he remarked, "Switzerland is so small, you know … you run into these people all the time at the train stations."

In a small family, everybody knows everybody else. How can you tell the truth when confronted with that worrisome fact? The question remains: How do you run a democracy and its justice system based on not offending friends? This mentality, of keeping secrets inside small circles because of negative repercussions to the family, is presumably also the reason why Switzerland chooses not to enact strong whistleblowers laws. The idea is to handle everything "within the family," whatever family that might be. And if you go beyond the family, you will be shunned.

There is a Swiss penchant for secrecy and for inducing shame in those who do go beyond the family circle with tales of wrongdoing. This attitude perhaps traces back to strict bank secrecy laws and the idea that wrongdoing concealed in that sector can be justified, because money and survival in a resource-poor country are at stake.

Combining small geographic size, relative

powerlessness and the claim of being resource-poor, we Swiss have created an anchor point and a likely reason to feel inadequate, thereby to look inward only and keeping things inside, and outside things away. The absence of a sense of power, whether this is imagined or real, leads to the perfection of other means to achieve ends, such as deception and manipulation.

***

There is, in Swiss society, a reticence—or perhaps more precisely stated a fear—of being too friendly or emotionally close that is often exquisitely perceived and commented on by outsiders. For example, Mormon missionary authorities, known for sending proselytizing youths all over the world, rank Switzerland among the top of the toughest fields for their work, psychologically.

I knew American missionaries who had been attacked by villagers with sticks and stones. And then I ran into a New Zealander who had married into a small, Swiss village in the Bernese Oberland. When I met her, she lamented that she had to leave her town and go back home to New Zealand for a time to regain a sense of personal warmth and humanity, as New Zealanders tend to be a gentle folk. She had been shunned by the locals as a newcomer and foreigner. Following recuperation back home, she returned to her husband in that same village, but with what she called "new expectations."

I recall an event from my youth: Having just moved to a new neighborhood in the USA, a neighbor knocked on our door with a pot of coffee, a welcoming gesture. My Swiss mother quickly told her to go away, essentially slamming the door in her face. It took years for her to discover that America was different, that strangers can be nice people, with reward to be had. In time, of course, she lost her fear and became happily "Americanized."

Talk spontaneously to a stranger on a tram or a bus here and you will be viewed with suspicion (but less so in Zermatt). Small talk between a stranger and many Swiss is plainly awkward. This type of behavior—talking to strangers without just cause—is commonly known and looked down on by the Swiss as typical "American-style superficial behavior." This superficiality contrasts with the prevailing myth that the Swiss, among themselves, engage with each other far more meaningfully.

The Swiss prefer to have lasting relationships with actual substance, they will inform an American. This may explain why a guest told me that, while his use of social media to gain a spontaneous and temporary partner for ice- and rock climbing activities always achieved results elsewhere, he never got even a single response to his requests in Switzerland. The often quoted "… but we Swiss are the most loyal, true-blue of friends once we accept someone as a friend" not withstanding here.

Trying to establish a relaxed, easy-going friendship with the Swiss can be like wrestling a buttered pig. You may think you have a firm hold, but wait one second. If you are the outsider, a spontaneous cup of tea and a quick chat will be hard to come by, and certainly not via an invitation to a Swiss home.

While tourists can expect and will undoubtedly receive gracious treatment for their short stays, easy familiarity is not on the Swiss menu with the cheese fondue. Of course, this clashes with the heartwarming Heidi fantasy created along with the breath-taking scenery.

I have often wondered and asked Swiss acquaintances why casual conversation with a stranger can't merely be viewed as a moment's diversion or simple entertainment. Why can't it be a trial for the beginning of a new friendship? I receive blank looks. This just isn't done. You already have friends whom you have known for thirty years, from your village. Especially meaningful relationships. That should be enough.

In fact, the Swiss would probably enjoy small talk if they allowed themselves, as Swiss who have lived abroad have discovered. They like and often remark kindly on the easy friendliness in other parts of the world, especially the USA, but it just doesn't work back home.

"When we come back here from overseas," a Swiss friend explained, "the shutters close down tight again." They do not know how to casually relate and still feel comfortable because they never learned and the culture does not encourage it. Small talk ranks right beside an understanding of irony on a list of absent Swiss social abilities. An ironic expression inevitably results in a look of downright confusion.

"Why do you call him curly, when he clearly has no hair?"

At the same time, American friends joke that the Swiss will come to your party, eat your cheese, drink your wine, then call the police at 10 p.m. because you're making too much noise! The 10 p.m. cut-off, by the way, is the ubiquitous, theoretical hour of necessary quiet, enforceable on occasion by law. Such behavior serves as proof that, if they did happen to reveal personal warmth with absolute strangers at a party, that can be retracted, the impression cleared from the mind before heading to bed at the end of the day. It's safer that way. Nothing of value has been traded for the possibly fleeting or insubstantial.

Sadly, there is adequate truth to all of this admittedly

horrible, anecdotal stereotyping. Stereotypes, after all, emerge from impressions and observations made again and again, then packaged for easy understanding. But I also have my support in this regard from other sources.

I recall a surprising comment made many years ago on a radio program, the *Larry King Show* if remembered correctly, by the owner of the *New York Times*. I can't recall the exact quote, but the paraphrase is something like this: *I have been all over the world, interacted with just about every known culture. There have only been one people that I could never really understand.*

At that point, I speculated that he would go on to refer to a tribe of savage primitives in the Amazon or headhunters in the highlands of New Guinea. But no, instead he went on to call out the Swiss. I took particular note of this comment because, after all, he was talking about my forbearers, my fellow countrymen.

Now, after living in Switzerland for fifteen years, I think I know what he meant.

Strength in Switzerland can still be measured the old-fashioned way, in a "strong and wrong beat weak and right" attitude, right along with the newly emerging authoritarianism as also practiced in modern, right-wing America. A holding back of expressed warmth and empathy, when the granting of such would provide comfort to a suffering soul, is embedded in a darker part of the psyche here. Shunning on a personal level is still practiced, as mentioned previously. It occurs even at the institutional level, by cutting off all communications.

Yes, the Swiss can shut down completely. A quick retreat into the mountainous redoubt of the Swiss mind produces a closing off—a means of protecting oneself, but also of showing dominance. Whoever gives in first in a contest of wills is the weaker. (Maybe the American lawyers will go home if we ignore them.) Down home, village-style hierarchy must be satisfied. As a first reaction to criticism that may disrupt that hierarchy, a successful "blame the victim" defense prevents a discomforting examination of whatever may be wrong.

The ubiquitous sense of powerlessness and shrinking from anything too overt or in the open in this culture has led to a certain refinement of psychological tactics and pressures imposed behind the scenes. You never get your ears pulled in public, because that would shame the family. However, when you finally get home alone, the law gets laid down.

"Switzerland is a curst selfish, swinish country of brutes, placed in the most romantic region of the world. I never could bear the inhabitants ..." Lord Byron wrote to Thomas Moore in 1821. This description of brutes in a swinish country certainly no longer applies. Nor, to be sure, the curst part. Mountains, glaciers, waterfalls and the inviting, flowered, cow- and goat-littered meadows do impress to the hilt, yes, and are exquisite natural resources. They pull in plenty of economic wealth, but they also inspire the souls of more than poets or romantics alone. That is where the confusion can come in. Just don't mix up the heart-warming scenery with warm hearts. The trick to surviving with one's expectations of human reciprocity intact is to find the exceptions, which I make into a necessary habit.

I will be remiss if I do not emphasize an important point along this rut-filled road, and perhaps I do so too late already, so for that I must apologize. I have been referring all along here to "the Swiss" as a monolith when, in fact, Switzerland is composed of three primary areas of language and culture, and a minor fourth. The area speaking the Swiss-German dialect is the largest, at sixty-two percent of the country, followed by the French and Italian areas, and the small Romansch-speaking area.

I have lived and presently live in the German part of Switzerland, which includes Zermatt, and I therefore should limit my experiences, descriptions and observations to mainly the Swiss-German-speaking part of Switzerland. There are obvious differences among the cultural regions. The French and Italian parts are said not to suffer from the same social strangulation as the Swiss-German-speaking region. This observation comes directly from the mouths of other Swiss who live in those areas, i.e. self-appraisal.

IV.   Swiss Trivia and Oddities

"I've learned that when someone does something very kind and refuses payment, giving them an engraved Swiss Army knife is never refused!"
~ Christine Lavin, singer, songwriter, guitarist and recording artist

The Swiss are iconic in that most everyone has heard of Switzerland and may have preconceived notions about the country. This book is speckled throughout with my impressions of "what makes the Swiss, Swiss." Here, I present some oddities and trivia in the tourists spirit that I hope will add to reader enjoyment or pique curiosity.

Checking out the hashtag #onlyinSwitzerland shows Twitter images of Swiss vending machines offering the polar opposite of junk food. Cheese, milk, yogurts and eggs are dispensed in place of candy bars and potato chips. Sugary soft drinks are consumed in less abundance here also.

While the Swiss enjoy their meat and cheese, healthy eating (at least for some) appears to be a "thing" according to www.livekindly.co, which dubs Switzerland as "the best country in Europe to be vegetarian." Guests can ask me for vegan recommendations and I provide suggestions on restaurants in Zermatt.

One can't help but wonder whether the tranquility of life and simple, solid Alpine food here had something to do with the intestinal fortitude of the oldest mountaineer to climb the Matterhorn, something he had done a total of 370 times! What an achievement for Ulrich Inderbinen, who was born in 1900 and died in 2004 at the age of one-hundred and four. He was eighty-nine years old (some say ninety) when he last scaled the Lady.

Many of my guests visit a newly-upgraded fountain in Zermatt honoring old Ulrich and his climbing prowess. He remained a mountain guide until age 96, when an injury on the Breithorn mountain finally stopped him.

It's a well-known fact that deaths due to bad weather, falls, crevices, falling rocks and plain bad luck are not uncommon around the Matterhorn—and Ulrich dodged all of those to achieve something noteworthy.

By the way, Dani Arnold broke the record in the fastest climb to the top of the north face of the Matterhorn—an 1,100 meter ascent (just over 3,600 feet). It takes average mountain climbers about four hours from the base to the top, yet Dani did it in just an hour and forty-six minutes, beating the last record-holder by ten minutes.

Another fun-fact meme on Instagram states: "Switzerland was founded in 1291 with the alliance of three small communities and its real name is Confoederatio Helvetica." Those three original territories are the cantons of Uri, Schwyz, and Unterwalden (the latter divided today into the cantons of Nidwalden and Obwalden).

This author was born in Uri, in the town of Altdorf, the home of the legendary William Tell, a crossbow marksman who is said to have assassinated a tyrant there when it was under the control of Habsburg dukes in the 13th century.

Thanks to Mr. Tell and others, we today have the only direct democracy on the planet. I wind up voting about five times per year. If they're going to cut down a tree in Zermatt, by God I want to have a say in it! That being said, the Swiss voting participation rate has been sinking steadily and is below 50%, ranking only 21st among nations in that regard, with the USA ahead by a nose.

There's a backstory to the name. Helvetia (or Helvecia) appears on certain Swiss coins as the symbol of Switzerland—in female form. In artwork, we see her holding a spear and a shield that displays the Swiss flag. Helvetia's wreath of braided hair symbolizes "confederation," and the Latin *Confoederatio Helvetica* translates to "the Swiss Confederation." Even today, the Swiss use the Latin in this reference.

Helvetica, the same-named font on our computers today, was invented by Swiss typeface designer Max Miedinger in 1957. And since we are speaking of computers, the mouse was co-invented by René Sommer, a Swiss programmer.

What other inventions can the Swiss claim? Well, *not* the cuckoo clock! Although often attributed to the Swiss, the Germans in the Black Forest region of southern Germany deserve credit for the design of the traditional forest-type cuckoo clock. Fear not, however, as even German cuckoo clocks will please uninformed tourists in Zermatt. You can find a rich assortment in local souvenir shops. Otherwise, well-known and authentically Swiss chalet-style cuckoo clocks are made by the Loetscher family of Switzerland in the Canton of Berne and are sold here. These artisans debuted their first clock in 1920 and will celebrate a one-hundred year anniversary in 2020.

The Swiss can claim aluminum foil (by Robert Victor Neher) and cellophane (by Jacques E. Brandenberger) as inventions, as well as Velcro by Swiss engineer George de Mestral.

Another Swiss creation? Absinthe, an aniseed-flavored liqueur traditionally derived from anise, fennel and the wormwood shrub. The strong, green concoction was supposedly imbibed by Pablo Picasso, Edgar Allen Poe, Ernest Hemingway and Vincent Van Gogh (who allegedly cut off his ear after drinking it). It was banned in 1910, but is now very much back in favor.

Swiss absinthe was briefly given protected status in Switzerland in 2012, which prevented foreign manufacturers from selling it under the same name. This restriction was reversed upon numerous appeals in 2014, but points to the Swiss proclivity for protecting their branding.

***

Odd Swiss town names—odd, at least, to an American ear—are scattered throughout the landscape. While traveling in Switzerland, you might also run across street names with the same or similar spelling:

- *Bad Egg* in Zurich
- *Frick* in the Canton of Aargau
- *Gland* in the Canton of Vaud
- *Misery-Courtion* in the Canton of Fribourg
- *Rain and Root* in the Canton of Lucerne
- *Gross* in the Canton of Schwyz
- *Bitsch* in the Canton of Vallais

A few quick, geographical facts that should be mentioned include the many countries that border Switzerland: Germany, Austria, France, Italy and tiny

Liechtenstein. Cantons are the twenty-six member regions that comprise the nation: Zürich, Bern, Luzern, Uri, Schwyz, Obwalden, Nidwalden, Glarus, Zug, Fribourg, Solothurn, Basel-Stadt, Basel-Landschaft, Schaffhausen, Appenzell Ausserrhoden, Appenzell Innerrhoden, St. Gallen, Grisons, Aargau, Thurgau, Ticino, Vaud, Valais, Neuchâtel, Geneva, and Jura.

Of course, there is a lot of international travel for business and tourism to all of these picturesque destinations. If you are one such traveler, perhaps you've seen the Zurich Airport advertisement: "Like shopping for a Swiss watch. Hard to make a mistake." Literally any canton features an attraction of interest to tourists.

This brings up Swiss watches, which have a global reputation for excellence. Why? Well, according to chief executive of the Swiss watchmaker IWC Schaffhausen, Georges Kern: "The Swiss have that image of producing quality at the highest level, as Germans have the image of producing the best cars in the world. And you cannot just copy this." (For the sake of accuracy if not image, we must mention that, for years, Japanese car manufacturers have consistently ranked above their German counterparts for reliability.)

A few more bits of trivia have bubbled to the surface in the quest to uncover curious Swiss lore. Children of the late 1930s and early 1940s may recall Radio Man, a.k.a. SABOR IV, an actual walking, talking, yodeling Swiss robot featured in Popular Science magazine in 1939. This particular robot was built by Swiss engineer August Huber of the Canton of Appenzell and should not be confused with the science fiction novel, *The Radio Man* by American writer Ralph Milne Farley.

The Swiss have notable monsters, most of them ancient, that are still a part of the culture. There's the

Böögg, which has evolved into an exploding, stuffed snowman in Zürich's Sechseläuten spring festival. The basilisk—a reptile-like creature—is the heraldic animal of Basel and appears in bridge artwork and fountains throughout the city. The Schnabelgeiss—a tall, horned spirit with a beak—allegedly appears during December's winter solstice and is driven out by the townsfolk in Ottenback as they disguise themselves and rattle wooden objects to drive the spirit away.

As someone who prides himself on rationality—as imagined as that might be— I am struck by the degree to which folklore persists in Switzerland, for example in stories involving the antics of such creatures as mentioned above. In this regard, for better or for worse, such references to legends or tradition or influences from a mythical spirit world on the contemporary were largely absent from my life growing up in Pittsburgh, USA.

Previously mentioned here was the mythological giant Gargantua and his accomplice Cervin, who formed the Matterhorn. There's also the Devil's Bridge in Uri, based on the legend that local villagers wanted to construct a stone bridge and paid a stranger—the devil— to do it for them. Payment for the service? The first soul to cross the bridge. So what did the clever villagers do? They sent across a goat, thus enraging the devil, who threw a rock to destroy the bridge, but missed. It landed in a canyon near Göschenen and can be seen by tourists today.

Try explaining the construction of the Golden Gate Bridge like this and find yourself quickly surrounded by sheriff's deputies. On the other hand, infrastructure in general is in outstanding condition and up-to-date in Switzerland, despite superstitions and myths. And in the USA …?

IV. Quaint and Traditional

"One of my favorite things to cook is fondue. I'm Swiss. It's a great social meal."
~ Ryan Seacrest, radio personality, television host, and producer

The foregoing having been said overall as my offering of a rough guide to human relations expectations in Switzerland, I do not sense the same level of coldness to the outsider here in Zermatt. I didn't know a soul when I first arrived, but my reception was warm. Nowhere else in Switzerland have I been approached by strangers and spoken to or asked about my opinion on this or that. The unusual population dynamics in Zermatt may explain this. Of the 5,700 permanent residents, about 3,000 are non-Swiss, primarily Portuguese but also Spanish, Greek, Italian. They work here and literally keep the place running as taxi drivers, construction workers, hospitality industry employees and so on. Then we also have a flux of seasonal workers, also foreigners.

Our village accommodates up to as many as 35,000 inhabitants in August, December or February with, in total, about three million visitors passing through per year as of 2018. Forty percent of visitors are Swiss, Germans come in second at 8.5%, Americans third (6.4%) Great Britain fourth (5.8%) and the Japanese fifth (3.5%). The year 2018 set a new record for overnight stays, at 2.2 million, up 6.2% compared to the previous year. I have personally greeted guests from over 40 countries.

We host all of these folks in a recognizably welcoming fashion, as the village provides a number of events and entertainment venues to keep our tourists happy. The locals welcome the heavy influx, except for the fact that taxes paid by locals also need to cover those times per year that include more than a five-fold increase in population, putting considerable strain on local services such as waste disposal and recycling.

In summer, we have a herd of about forty-five blackneck goats stride gracefully and proudly from one end of our village to the other, twice a day, at 9 a.m. and 5 p.m., forth and back, escorted by local schoolchildren who dare you to find anything more cute or traditional or Swiss-like. This may seem a simple attraction, but it is one that pays off mightily in terms of good will toward this village, and happy memories. The crowds love this quaint bit of Switzerland. Follow the goats and you will also see flocks of smiling foreigners, grinning ear to ear, concentrating intensely on their next photo.

Quaint and traditional—that is what tourists like these days. But where does tradition end and fear of, or resentment of, change begin? I often have reason to wonder about that in Switzerland.

You can find the oddest, most perplexing mix of the modern with the seemingly outdated or even irrational in Switzerland. Air conditioning is a rarity, even in five-star hotels. Another modest but telling example is a lack of screens on windows and screen doors in Swiss homes, shops and hotels. No shortage of winged creatures enter dwellings, not least flies when they tire of goats. Window treatments are universally completely modern and in excellent structural condition, thus the lack of screens has been a puzzle to me ever since I arrived in Switzerland.

Recently, I went into a bakery to buy a slice of

delicious apricot pie. To my amazement, within the clean, modern glass service counter I spotted four pieces of pie (apple, apricot, rhubarb and rhubarb again), each featuring its own, live wasp, merrily dancing above or crawling right on the sugary delicacies.

Gobsmacked, I warned the salesperson, "Hey, there are wasps on these pieces of pie!"

"I know," she explained calmly. "There is nothing we can do about that."

I gazed at her, speechless.

Now, lest a reader get the wrong impression, this was not some dilapidated bakery that had seen better days, teetering at the edge of bankruptcy. It was on the main street of Zermatt, meticulously appointed and perfect in every way... except that it had no screen door—the easy, sure solution to the problem of wasps when the front door is kept open in warm weather.

Screens are not a digital-age invention, nor do they arise from the recent space age. But since no one has ever had window screens or a screen door, apparently no one will ever have window screens or a screen door. It's tradition. And if you do not like that, go get your apricot pie elsewhere, where there are no wasps or flies!

Yet ... at the same time in other fields, the Swiss will be the first to employ new technology. They were using fax machines, for example, before they became common in Milwaukee, where I lived at that time.

And don't get me started on Swiss sidewalks in winter. This is the one area where I can see a benefit to the existence of ... lawyers. The Swiss tend to ignore icy, snowy sidewalks, as if they did live in Tahiti. How is this possible when it violates all of the instincts of perfection and cleanliness so evident in other areas? To this day, I ask myself this question.

Remarkable as it may seem, the Swiss have not learned the lesson well known in Milwaukee, Minneapolis, Chicago and Buffalo: if you remove snow quickly, it will not form a sheet of ice that becomes almost impossible to remove and treacherous to pedestrians. The only answer that I have received when I ask about this omission is the lame defense that each individual should be responsible for his or her own safety, if you don't get a blank stare for daring to ask the question in the first place.

How many older folks break hips, legs, arms here on icy sidewalks? If there is such a statistic, it will probably remain undiscoverable. If they did let American lawyers in here, which is as likely as Heidi doing free lap dances at the five-star luxury, stately Zermatterhof Hotel, Swiss bank accounts might rapidly approach those of Americans.

***

In August of 2018, Zermatt hosted its first *Ringkuhkampf*, a summer cow fighting competition, or the so-called Combat of the Queens. This is no bull; this matchup is no stranger to other Swiss villages, but first time here. Two hoofed milk-givers are put together in a confined space for the express purpose of fighting each other for dominance, the prevailing cow then proclaimed the winner.

Now, it must be plainly stated that these placid cows normally have absolutely no desire to fight. They are Swiss, after all. When I examined the rules for the fight, I was mightily amused to see that if a particular cow refuses to fight, she is considered a "loser." What? For a nation that often refuses to fight (frequently for good reason, sometimes not), is it not too parsimonious of spirit to call the cow that wishes to remain neutral a loser? She, like the nation, may be smart enough not to waste energy when it makes no sense, like in this case for the amusement of Swiss hillbillies.

I'll save my strength for producing milk for chocolate or help my children become veal cutlets, the "loser" may well be thinking.

VI.   Sightseeing and Village Life

I had rather be first in a village than second at Rome.
~ Julius Caesar

Zermatt has no industry outside of tourism and mountain sports. The village is not economically viable in any other sense. Tourists are our lifeblood, and this plays out even as dueling weather forecasts.

If you are a meteorologist working for Google, stay out of Zermatt; we really hate you. Reason? Google weather forecasts present images of clouds and precipitation for even the slightest threat of a drop of rain. This, the locals claim, needlessly prevents people from coming to the village. To counter this threat to survival, Zermatt tourism presents its own forecast often showing abundant sunshine. Having paid close attention to these warring factions, I claim that both are inaccurate, but surely Google more so. Let's just say that the Google forecasters are "less optimistic."

When Google weather doesn't scare folks away, there is always the Swiss folk music that plays at the train station and along the main street from time to time in summer, including the mandatory alphorns—music guaranteed to help you fall asleep, one step closer to that coveted meditation you have been attempting to master for so long. Of course, again the tourists are mesmerized by the quaintly dressed musicians and the strange absence of rap lyrics. Cows, on the other hand, have heard too much and can be seen shaking their heads.

One aspect of culture that remains ever popular in Zermatt is music. Apart from the Swiss folk music at the train station and along the main street, musicians from all over the world arrive to play concerts here. Groups of student musicians make their way into town throughout the summer, sweeping through in the form of one wave after another.

For children, a main attraction might be Wolli, the local, black-faced sheep mascot with human locomotion inside. He (it) offers a warm welcome to everyone right at the train station or as he wanders around the town. His relatives on four legs (300 of them) may also be visited in their ultra-clean, modern sheep barn residence a slight ways up the mountain.

Abundant souvenir shops carry the usual merchandise associated with Switzerland. Some of it is even made in Switzerland. Practically every major Swiss watch brand has an outlet in Zermatt. No problem buying a diamond-encrusted watch for 600,000 Swiss francs in town. There are also upper-end fashion shops like Boegner, Ogier and Moncler.

The shops, hotels and restaurants that line the main street in close array are mostly dark-timbered, three- to six story chalet-like structures with amply flowered balconies and colorful shutters, no concrete or steel monoliths and no garish advertising or neon signs allowed.

I personally visit and find of particular interest three business establishments in Zermatt. One is *Andy's Musikshop,* which, in practice, is really an art and poster shop, as that comprises 90% of the shop's contents. It's a two-minute walk from the train station to a miniature mall across the main street.

Andy has been running the same shop in the same

location for forty-five years ... pretty impressive. He carries a varied, well-presented and colorful assortment of lithographs, posters, abstract and fine art works and traditional landscape oil paintings around the themes of Zermatt, skiing, and mountains. Being situated next to the most frequented grocery store in town, Andy winds up waving to—or shouting at—much of the population of locals as they stop in, wave or shout back at him as they pass by.

I also escort guests to *The Art Gallery*, an artist's workshop and fine art gallery exhibiting the eclectic works of local artist Lucas Davis and various guest artists who rotate seasonally. The architecture of the building, with its superb blend of stone, wood and glass inside and out, was nominated for a Swiss architectural award and makes a visit worthwhile. A bonus that comes with visiting the gallery is its location along a quiet, historic cobblestoned passageway in the old village, dating back four hundred years—close by, yet far enough from the highly commercialized main street to be old-village silent.

***

While years ago few people wanted things that were traditional, we are now tired of everything being the same everywhere. There seems to be a "going back" to roots and tradition as in local versus global. Even the Romansh language, the fourth official Swiss language spoken by fewer than 0.5% of the population and only in the Canton of Graubünden, is making a comeback today.

A McDonald's restaurant is the only fast-food restaurant chain in town. It managed to open in this conservative village after what I was informed was a lengthy court battle. The last thing the numerous local, full-service restaurants want is fast-food joints lining the main Bahnhofstrasse. And no Starbucks. Instead, we do have Stephanie's crepes shop, a half-underground hole-in-the-wall gem on Main Street where Stephanie slaves away, happily preparing delicious crepes in front of your eyes and for the long line of tourists who just as happily wait patiently outside for theirs, since only about four people fit seated inside the place.

From June to August, the main Bahnhofstrasse offers street food while a D.J. plays music in the center of town to fuel a street party scene, including exuberant dancing on the main street. Restaurants and bars open their sliding/folding front windows and a sense of warm community gets into full swing.

Of course, tourists bring with them treasure, not the problems of permanent settlement. That, as is usual in Switzerland, is strictly limited. For example, there was the infamous Swiss village of Oberwil-Lieli in the Canton of Aargau that preferred to pay a penalty of 300,000 Swiss francs rather than welcome refugees. A few years back, the Pope called on Catholic parishes throughout the world to accept one refugee family each. In Zermatt, that entreaty from on high seems to have been ignored, and it should be no surprise.

When I asked a local priest about this, he quickly changed the subject, explaining that he had helped an undocumented refugee obtain paperwork—presumably to live somewhere else but not Zermatt. Along this line, the Swiss voted some years back to ban the new construction of minarets (but not mosques) in what was, no doubt, less than a serious blow to jihadists, but adequate reason to ask... what, exactly, are the Swiss afraid of and how did that measure help?

***

It may be a surprising fact, but a tourist can visit Zermatt and encounter few or even no Swiss natives. The conductors on the trains coming through the narrow valley are probably native, but they may also be German. Dining in a restaurant or staying at a hotel? German or Italian waiters and other foreign staff are most likely at your service. Souvenir shop purchase? You could be buying from an Asian salesperson. Heading up to the base of the Matterhorn on the cable car? Your ticket can be handed to you by a Brit or a Dutchman or a person from just about any other country. Even the ski instructors and mountain guides are often non-Swiss.

A five-star hotel just aside my location employs workers from every part of Europe. Rarely have I seen a native Swiss hotel worker on the service staff. The top management, however, is certainly Swiss, as is highly likely the case elsewhere in town.

As far as basic necessities of life are concerned, all are available in Zermatt, of course. We do need to cater to people with refined tastes in fashion and food for the short periods of their vacations. But selection in many categories can nevertheless be limited.

We count on three full-line, average-fare grocery stores and one smaller, quick-mart type shop for daily needs. There are two butcher shops and a bunch of excellent bakeries all over town. Surprisingly, there are no cheese shops per se. Good cheeses can be purchased at the grocery store.

Despite Zermatt's reputation and expectations to the contrary, prices for food here are basically no higher than anywhere else in Switzerland. Suffice it to say, they are high enough everywhere else in Switzerland. As is well known, Switzerland is not a low-cost country.

While selection may be limited in other areas of commerce, that will not be the case for mountain-related sportswear, outdoor equipment or ski instructors and mountain guides. On the main street alone, there must be ten sportswear and sporting good shops within a ten-minute walk, plus the Zermatters Alpine Center catering to adventurous outdoor tastes.

Regarding photography—as there is a law preventing the flying of drones within five kilometers of an airport or, in our case here, a heliport—my guests are prevented from flying their camera-laden drones over the village, which they are sorely tempted to do from my balcony.

I had a guest who once claimed that he took more than a thousand photos in three days—not from a drone, but with his hand-held camera. In the days of Kodak, this might have cost a pretty penny. Interestingly, the only photo shop in town closed down several years ago.

Another guest not long ago asked me to show her the spot where her mother had been photographed forty years earlier, with the Matterhorn as the prominent backdrop. I recognized her photo immediately. It was taken at the popular *Kirchenbrücke,* the bridge at the church in the center of town, with perhaps the most iconic view of the Matterhorn in the village. Rain or shine, day or evening, you will find amateur and professional photographers assembled there, tripods deployed, waiting for just the right lighting. The spot has become so popular, in fact, that the village is erecting a dedicated viewing platform next to the banks of the Vispa River, to ease the crowding along the bridge.

When we arrived at my guest's spot, a five-minute walk away from my home, we compared the photo she had brought along from the past to the current reality. It was clear, humans came and went while Nature had taken little notice. Surely, the Matterhorn must be among the world's most photographed mountains, if not itself in first place.

In the fall of the year and with some luck—for a few days depending on the winds—a photographer might be able to capture an extraordinary view of the iconic Matterhorn while the larch forest is still intact in green. Brilliant gold pops out here and there practically overnight, a scattering of broad-leafed trees not noticeable at other times in the green sea.

My favorite hike is along a trail that passes under a rare patch of what most locals call birch trees, but in fact an examination of the bark and leaves verifies aspen, remindful of the Utah or Colorado variety.

In the wind, thousands of yellow leaves flutter, each to an erratic tune, dancing to their own beat. The effect is dazzling, like looking at a ring entrusted with tiny diamonds, the eye cannot help but dance along.

Stopping on the trail before this patch of aspen, it is impossible to see the Matterhorn above except through this screen of fireflies. Part of the beauty of this scene is that it is rare. The wind that causes the phenomenon is also the source of its destruction. Come a few days late and see merely leafless skeletons. Should the sun be blocked by clouds for a few days, the scene passes for ordinary, if being under the Matterhorn can be ordinary.

Another Alpine tree here, the Swiss stone pine, (Pinus cembra) might also easily be confused with the piñon pine of the American Southwest, due to its wonderfully aromatic fragrance. The Swiss claim that a room paneled with this wood lowers heart rate and diminishes anxiety. I do not doubt this, as burning it in hotel fireplaces also has a mellowing effect on those who are drawn to it.

VII.   Tourism and the Great Outdoors

*"The Matterhorn—mystical, majestic, the mountain of mountains.
No one can escape its fascination. Neither locals nor guests."*
~ Zermatt Tourism (surprise!)

Zermatt is a tourist magnet within a tourist magnet—Switzerland. Neither disappoints in offerings both material and natural.

By far most of our shops and many sources of activities in Zermatt are concentrated right along the main street, named the Bahnhofstrasse (what else would it be called in Switzerland?) as it more or less parallels the nearby Vispa River—a mountain stream really—flowing through the length of Zermatt and carrying some of the ever-increasing runoff from melting snow or glaciers above.

Within a fifteen minute walk, the Bahnhofstrasse extends from the train station at one far end of town, through the center of town activities, past an excellent museum that recreates the Zermatt of old and tells the story of the first ascent of the mountain—long before Winston Churchill climbed it in his youth—past the town square and a physically imposing, spired church, then a small, rushing mountain stream, up a slight incline and on to the cable car lift and Matterhorn Glacier Paradise, a main ski and hiking area.

In May and November, the population in Zermatt may drift downward to around 4,000 as the locals go on vacation for the offseason—commercial downtime—but uptime for construction work. Helicopters whirr through the village sky and crisscross the valley throughout those months with cargoes that dangle from their bellies and abruptly drop down like spiders from a web. They may suddenly wind up hovering overhead, lowering and lifting building materials over and onto nearby chalet roofs for ever-ongoing commercial renovations. Among their other good qualities, the Swiss keep things well up to date and visually tidy.

These helicopters, flying from the village heliport, also serve for tourist flights around the Matterhorn and proudly in the vital function of mountain rescue for climbers and skiers and anyone else who may get into trouble in the heights. To be sure, injury and death in the mountains are not rare here. The copters ferry the injured and sick to the nearest hospital, about ten minutes by air versus an hour or more otherwise. Before that, however, several doctors always in town can provide emergency services.

As is true in other places, like the Grand Canyon for example, helicopter jockeys like to fly visitors on excursions into the surrounding mountains, the more the merrier. And like everywhere else, the ensuing noise and disturbance lead to calls for less crass commercialism. Good luck with that. Zermatt tourism isn't here to promote the restriction of activities that lure visitors. Like everywhere else, lovers of Nature have an uphill battle against commercial interests.

***

Tourist largess and mountain sports keep us all afloat in Zermatt. In addition to summer hiking, both a cogwheel train and a cable car take bicycles uphill, the tourists themselves must figure out how to get them back down without disfiguring any sheep.

There is also a forest fun park for children and adults that offers safe climbing to treetop level with safety harnesses at the edge of town, right below the Matterhorn.

The mountains in general and the Lady herself are, of course, the real attraction in Zermatt. There is a joke that is told: What would the village of Zermatt be without Lady Matterhorn? Answer: Saas-Fee. This quip comes at the expense of a neighboring village, Saas-Fee, that also offers fine skiing, good vistas and peaks to climb or otherwise ascend, but it has no special claim to fame and thus far fewer tourists. Unlike us, it is just one more fairly ordinary Swiss ski resort.

In summer, Zermatt mountain guides will offer to take physically fit individuals to the top of the Matterhorn for around 1,500 Swiss francs. Climbing experience is not necessarily a prerequisite. In August, the most popular month for mountain touring, internationally licensed mountain guides from various countries congregate at the popular Brown Cow tavern in the center of town, about two minutes from my place, hoping to lure some of the estimated, annual three thousand Matterhorn conquerors.

I ran into several American guides from Colorado who offered their services here a few hundred francs cheaper and promised to be more patient, leaving more time for photo taking than their Swiss competitors, they claimed.

The Matterhorn, I am told, is not a difficult mountain to climb technically, but if you decide to scale it with any of the guides, you may first need to prove your stamina on a less challenging mountain. No refund on the amount paid in advance if you peter out and must forego the Matterhorn.

A recent guest made it two thirds of the way to the top of the Matterhorn with his guide, only to be told that his footwork appeared too insecure to continue to the summit. Continuing without a guide could have been dangerous. The guest had to abandon the mountain, no refund. Shortly thereafter, another guest, an officer in the British Navy who was not an experienced mountaineer, did make it to the top, but exclaimed that is was far more difficult than he had imagined.

Little expense is spared in dressing up the mountains here to seduce the hordes. The autumn of 2018 saw the introduction of a new, fantastic cableway that operates all year round and carries up to two thousand passengers per hour from the Glacier Paradise area upward to the adjacent Klein (small) Matterhorn peak. A portion of this ride includes the world's highest 3S cableway—a Swiss-invented, three-cable cabin transport system—that connects an intermediate station (the Trockener Steg) with a station at a whopping 3,883 meters. It's called the "Crystal Ride" because the gondolas were specially finished by the Swarovski crystal folks to include "crystal rocks"—a first for a cable car—in addition to leather seats.

Lest you think that such adornments are superfluous, some think otherwise. I once asked a German guest, a head stewardess for a major airline, if she enjoyed her stay in Zermatt and whether she would like to return someday.

"No," my guest stated flatly and firmly.

"Why not?" I asked in surprise.

"Because … the ski lift seats here aren't heated. In Austria, all the ski lift seats are heated."

"Oh" I remarked. So much for me thinking we were perfect. I left it at that. Recently I was told that our new lift seats were now also heated.

**

A comparison with the North American Rockies reveals that the Rockies and the Alps are similar in elevation, but ski towns in the Alps are often located at lower elevations and the skiing tends to run longer, with a more vertical drop. Aspen, Colorado, has its longest ski run in the States at about five miles (eight km). In Zermatt, the longest ski run is twelve miles. The average run in Colorado has 3,000 or 4,000 feet of vertical drop, while Swiss runs can be as much as 8,000 feet (2,500 m).

Because of differences in climate, Swiss trees stop growing as low as 7,500 feet (2,300 m). In parts of the Colorado Rockies trees will continue to grow even as high as 11,000 feet (3,350 m). Thus, skiers get more time above tree line in the Swiss Alps and in Zermatt.

When our larch trees have given up their rust-red and orange dress, decorative Christmas lighting kicks in along main street, abruptly breaking the blackness and bleakness of late fall. If, to savor the offerings, you happen to be booked at either of the two old and stately five-star hotels along the Bahnhofstrasse, the Mount Cervin or the Zermatterhof, you and your luggage will be invited to take the two-minute trip to either hotel via a two-horse drawn carriage, complete with sleigh bells, both winter and summer. I once offered an apple to one of the pair of horses as they waited at the train station, appearing quite bored. The driver approached me when he saw what I was about to do and instructed, "You need to cut that apple and give each one a half. Otherwise, they get jealous."

Who knew?

The centrally located, five-star Zermatterhof Hotel also gears up for the onrush of visitors with its unique outdoor ice bar, constructed by using monstrous blocks of fully transparent ice that accommodate magnum bottles of Champaign and wine encased firmly within. The parties are in full swing then, indoors and out.

Winters here basically begin at the Christmas season and lead into the other main occupations besides gawking at Lady Matterhorn—skiing and snowboarding. Unlike North America, in Switzerland skiing includes more than just skiing; it includes eating and drinking and the après-ski scene as well. In Zermatt, we have about eighty restaurants and other minor refueling stations on the surrounding mountains, outside of town. Eating fondue from a bubbling hot pot in a mountain hut along a ski route, with coffee or various alcoholic beverages, is all a part of what we know as skiing, here in Switzerland.

***

If ever there were a place suited to ignoring the problems of the world, Zermatt would be that place. How far would one need to travel to see poverty or misery or political turmoil? Or to be reminded of climate change, at least in terms of temperatures too hot? Yes, the glaciers are melting, but only scientists and a few locals take much notice; the glaciers still look big to tourist. And, because we are one mile high, temperatures never get too extreme here either, though definitely much above normal lately.

Concerns here about despots off-the-handle or

heading off the cliff and tweeting wildly, or unwanted immigration? Elsewhere, or maybe across the border and many kilometers away over a high mountain pass. I'm not sure. But surely not evident here in Zermatt!

***

Another point of congregation that I like here, the third of my favorite shops, is *Air-Taxi,* the paragliding office and school. I send my guests who wish to enjoy paragliding with the ultimate concern for safety to see Bruno, the owner, instructor and chief pilot. Bruno is conservative and a master at preventing his customers from feeling butterflies just before takeoff.

For safe paragliding, conservative is exactly what you want and need. Wind changed and no longer just right when you get to one of several destinations for takeoff? Well, sorry, you will have to go back down and try another time (no fee charged).

There are a number of jump-off points in Zermatt for what statistically is the very safe sport of paragliding. Insurance rates for tandem tourist paragliding, the best indicator of safety, reflect this. No training is required for tandem flying; no one is too heavy, too young or too old. Dogs have even tagged-along (cats are not welcome).

Dozens of my guests have flown with Bruno from sites on-high ranging from about 2,000 meters to 3,800 meters (6,500 to 12,500 feet). The Matterhorn and various glaciers and other peaks are always in birds-eye view during a flight. Flying time can range from about twenty minutes to close to an hour, depending on conditions. Asked to describe their experiences with Bruno on a scale of one to ten, the responses from my guests range almost always from ten to eleven.

The paragliding shop also attracts passersby, as mountain sports enthusiasts of all sorts, local and otherwise, stop in to say hello to Bruno and swap stories.

In Zermatt, opportunities to express physical courage in adrenalin-charged activities abound. This draws mountain men and women from all parts. We are a sort of mandatory destination for true mountain- and winter sports enthusiasts from all over the world, like a trip to the Vatican if you're Catholic. You can meet these folks, along with celebrities of various sorts, from time to time here. And you can even run into somewhat more infamous types.

VIII.   A Fugitive in Zermatt?

"I live in a Swiss village so small, if you sneeze everyone knows."
~ Geraldine Chaplin, daughter of Charlie Chaplin

And so, how did I end up in my mountainside retreat, which looms over most of the village below, with spectacular views of towering peaks in two directions, east and north? It was pure luck that I found the place—my little bit of paradise that also boasts two balconies, one in each of those directions.

A woman had been showing me a dreary apartment half below ground on the other side of town.

"No, I'm sorry," I explained. "I have to have some sunshine."

"Well, my nephew may have something for you, then; let me phone him," she offered.

She did so and I took it.

I expected to pay a hefty security deposit—three months is not unusual in Switzerland. But the landlord turned out to be a jewel. He was exceptionally friendly and welcoming from the first, acting unlike what I often encountered elsewhere. He was casual and at ease, showed no great interest in the financial arrangements or the strict application of rules for the sake of the rules. He managed a small shop in the middle of town and belonged to one of several established, old-line families of the village. He was my first anchor as a newcomer.

At first I wondered whether my landlord would object to accommodating Airbnb guests, which only occurred to me after I fully savored the beauty of my new location. His welcoming, open-minded attitude in large part encouraged me to do so. As fortune provided, my building was also zoned specifically to host tourists, a fact not unusual in a village where eighty percent of the dwellings are intended just for that purpose.

After deciding that inviting guests would ease the loneliness that I felt following the death of my close friend in Interlaken, and knowing I had the perfect location, my first hurdle was filling-in the Airbnb application form to become an official host. This is where the situation became somewhat tricky. You see, I had a slight problem that had followed me for some time—my history back in the United States.

***

Cue the international intrigue and allow me to reveal the secret that I've been keeping. I, your Airbnb host, scholar, editor and author, am classified by the United States as a fugitive felon, or at least so I was. Yes, I was labeled a criminal, a fugitive from justice, as proclaimed specifically by U.S. Marshalls in the City of Milwaukee, Wisconsin. Not only that, I was also categorized as "armed and dangerous." As if that were not bad enough, a Red Notice alert had been issued for me throughout the world by Interpol, the international policing organization. In short, I was the worst of the worst, and hardly an Airbnb host candidate, if the information as published were believed to be so.

Why were USA authorities after me?

The fact is, I had had no criminal history anywhere, let alone a history of violence. My problems with U.S. law and lawyers began after I started writing and publishing essays on a dysfunctional legal system in Milwaukee—explained in detail in a previous book, *Beyond Outrage* (www.beyond-outrage.com).

A child, my son, had been repeatedly and deliberately harmed, including having his head forced under water as punishment for loving his father. I knew of too may instances of postpartum depression leading to tragedy, even death. I wasn't going to allow that to happen; I stopped that harm, but in the process I also exposed the lawyers and police who had helped to conceal it in order to protect themselves and colleagues from criticism.

Essays that I published revealing the corruption led to considerable positive local notoriety among the citizenry, but they caused great anger among my targets. I had included the names of major figures involved in legal system corruption: lawyers, a local judge and a federal judge, among others. The essays eventually became my first book, *Beyond Outrage*, and a reason for my enemies to seek revenge.

I was sued for libel in Milwaukee and subsequently owed the largest sum of money ever awarded against an author in the State of Wisconsin, today well over one-million dollars. That legal action had taken place while I was out of the country, visiting New Zealand. The result was a default legal judgment, with me absent for the hearing, and unrepresented. I was not aware that the hearing had taken place until I read about it in a Milwaukee online newspaper.

When I refused to stop writing about the corruption that I had witnessed and the responsible individuals, the sum that I owed for libel continued to climb, as I had been prohibited by the court in Milwaukee from disclosing the story further. Tax problems soon followed, along with demands for large sums of money from a lawyer who had sued me. This was ultimately my motivation to return to Switzerland.

The Red Notice alert that had been issued for me, I discovered, puts law enforcement on notice internationally that an individual is wanted for arrest for crimes in a specific country. When I researched what this Interpol notice meant for me in practice for further travel, I discovered that Interpol is not itself a police force, but a means of assisting law enforcement in member nations by providing information on the whereabouts of international fugitives or persons wanted by law.

Of greater interest and relevance, I also learned that Interpol could be and was not infrequently misused for purely political purposes. For example, the Russian government was said to cause Interpol to issue Red Notices to target and bag political dissidents as they traveled. Former USA Ambassador to Russia, Michael McFaul, a critic of Russia, told an MSNBC interviewer that he feared being harassed by Russia by means of an Interpol notice while he traveled. I was certainly no such high profile personality, but what McFaul described was akin to what was intended for me as I traveled, courtesy of influential USA lawyers, not the Russians.

"You can't trust countries like Nigeria or Belarus not to misuse the criminal justice system and Interpol to advance corruption," commented Jago Russell, head of Fair Trials International, a rights group based in London that has been pushing Interpol to implement stronger safeguards. He might well have added the USA to his list.

In an ironic twist of fate, as I was writing this book the Chinese government announced that it had arrested and was holding the head of Interpol itself, Mr. Meng Hongwei, on charges of … taking bribes and corruption!

The exposure of corruption in Milwaukee was so detrimental to careers there that the U.S. Marshalls were somehow inveigled into characterizing me as "armed and dangerous" on their website, and then they involved Interpol, the exact procedure for which raising some questions. How do you claim someone is armed and dangerous when that person has no criminal or violent history, nor ever owned a gun?

The following report in the *New York Times* in March of 2019 may explain: "… amid a flurry of negative press coverage, Interpol began reviewing its red notice system in 2014. (…) It took another two years, but Interpol approved an overhaul that tightened records requirements, added a data protection officer and strengthened the internal review commission."

Interpol had failed to check my actual criminal history, presumably trusting Milwaukee authorities that acted on behalf of vengeful lawyers. The categorization was done falsely, in recoil to the fact that I dared use the First Amendment of the U.S. Constitution directly against lawyers with considerable influence. I had engaged freedom of truthful speech to interfere in the usual workings of a legal system gone badly wrong there.

Surely I had never been armed. What about dangerous? Well, that depends; the pen is mightier than the sword. My essays were dangerous enough that lawyers in Milwaukee concerned for their careers stepped over the line and common sense to involve Interpol. If this weren't a case of the misuse of Interpol, then what was? I set about to expose the injustice while living in Switzerland, where writing became my weapon and salvation but, again, eventually also a problem.

The above, abbreviated account was my history of fleeing the USA after deciding I was not going to pay the lawyer who sued me, and by doing so angered a number of important people with financial interests.

I explained the circumstances of my appearance in Switzerland to the Swiss police immediately upon my arrival in Interlaken. The higher echelons of the Swiss legal system exhibited surprising and complete disinterest in my story and the arrest warrant issued in Milwaukee, never mind any Red Notice by Interpol for the offense of writing about corrupt American lawyers. After all, no one here was shocked to discover legal system corruption in the USA. In fact they expected it. That suited me just fine. I had official blessing to stay in the country of my birth.

Some time after arriving in Switzerland, I had cause to phone the police chief in Interlaken. He had not been involved with upper management decisions on my arrival; he had never heard of me nor my strange history. I asked him if he could help me determine whether Interpol still had a Red Notice alert issued for me before I went on a planned trip outside the country.

He said, "You know, you, yourself, should be aware of whether you have done anything wrong."

I remained silent as I considered this unexpected response. Did the chief mean, by extension of his logic, that if I had done nothing wrong that would of necessity indicate that there was no Red Notice alert issued for me? Obviously, the man would have been mightily confused if I had tried to explain that there is such a thing as legal system corruption in the outside world, if not in his own village, that there are corrupt lawyers and local law enforcement will, in fact, aid those corrupt lawyers. I didn't even try.

To a large extent, Switzerland is still a country governed by a village mentality and guarded from some (not all) evil occurrences common elsewhere. Without doubt, what happened in my past in Milwaukee would have made little sense to this village police chief. And even if I could have convinced him that I was treated unjustly and unfairly in the USA, I would have been highly suspect for another reason important especially in Switzerland. Bucking the hierarchy in such an audacious way as I had done? Publishing essays? Books? Leaving a jurisdiction abroad illegally? Openly critical of authority? Not illegal here in Switzerland, but reason enough to suspect someone and to keep a healthy distance.

**

Once firmly established in Switzerland, I lobbied hard to convey my true history, especially at the University of Basel, where I worked as an instructor and proofer/editor in the chemistry department, and through the use of social media. I continued to write essays for publication from Switzerland, explaining how politics led to the misuse not only of an Interpol notice but also of law enforcement mechanisms in Milwaukee. Somewhere along the way, Interpol realized that they had been exploited, this time by the United States and Milwaukee. The Red Notice was withdrawn. However, I was still left struggling with damaging fake news about my history on the internet.

These were the unusual circumstances surrounding the frightening information associated with my name following a Google search, gladly brought to you by burned Milwaukee lawyers. In considering what my reactions should be to such information, first and foremost I didn't feel like a criminal; I wasn't hiding in Switzerland. I traveled freely throughout Europe.

Switzerland was now my home for practical reasons. From day one, Swiss authorities had never viewed me as a criminal. The opposite, in fact, was the case in their eyes.

Not so everywhere, however. My work at the University of Basel had been highly successful, indeed too successful. I was making news; I produced and directed well-publicized scientific research topics to the general public at theaters in Basel. The authorities in Milwaukee were not amused by this activity, as there was no harmony between their pronouncements of my evil nature and my employment at a Swiss university. They continued their internet attacks with false information and pressured the university about employing a criminal from the United States. Extradition to the USA, as some suggested would be my fate, was out of the question. Swiss citizenship made extradition practically impossible.

I forgive any reader at this point for thinking, *Wait a minute … this sounds just a bit too crazy. It's beyond belief.*

Indeed, let us agree that it is beyond belief. But being beyond belief doesn't mean it isn't true. And that fact is a major reason why I decided to write this book.

It is said that truth is stranger than fiction. There is a good reason for that being so. With good fiction, unless it is science fiction, an author must remain within the bounds of reader believability or risk losing them. Plausibility depends on what average readers have experienced or heard of, rather than on what might actually be possible. So the boundaries are set. But the truth has no such limits.

I was said by highly influential people in Milwaukee law enforcement to be one frightening thing; I needed to show the world that I was another thing.

As an author censored by lawyers in USA, and as a science editor and translator who had earned a living with countless projects related to the written word for years, I naturally gravitated to a writers' organization here, the Swiss-German PEN Centre, self proclaimed as serving "persecuted writers in Switzerland." It is a member organization of PEN International, which "promotes literature and defends the freedom of expression."

I met the criteria for membership in Swiss-German PEN, but I also wrote essays critical of a Swiss university that had eventually fallen under the spell of corrupt lawyers back in the USA and their fake news.

The Swiss prefer villains to be foreigners. Internal criticism causes anxiety and existential concerns. The Swiss-German PEN organization reflected the national ethos regarding criticism of anything Swiss. The Swiss need to live within a limited confine, meeting the same people continually, as previously noted. Tribalism runs deep and I was not a part of the tribe; I was the outsider, come to make trouble via the Americans.

When Swiss-German PEN discovered that my writing contained elements critical of, for one, how American lawyers influenced a Swiss university, I was disinvited from joining their organization. Allowing me to join would have been legitimizing criticism of people they knew. It was easier for Swiss-German PEN to raise concerns about exiled Turkish authors, for example, who had suffered censorship in Turkey, than to start looking inside the kitchen cupboards here.

I also began to wonder whether the Swiss reputation as one of the least corrupt nations might arise from pressures exerted internally to conceal troubling information through a combination of shunning, blame the victim, and censorship, but done cleverly so as not to be seen as such by the world.

IX.   Believe it ... or Not

We are born believing. A man bears beliefs as a tree bears apples.
~ Ralph Waldo Emerson

If the U.S. authorities label you a criminal, you should please the audience by acting like one. Otherwise you create confusion. I read that the American actor, Cam Gigandet, lamented that "It's such a challenge to play a good guy—it's hard to be believable." Amen to that.

I struggled with the burden of trying to explain my true but bizarre history for many years in Switzerland. Google information about me ruined professional relationships and employment. Friendships became practically impossible. Dating the opposite sex, once as easy as asking someone out for dinner, became virtually impossible.

If I am required to provide my last name during a personal interaction or introduction, I mispronounce it, or I follow its use with at least a short explanation or warning that a Google search will cause anxiety. This is the best that I can do. The results of these attempts at preemptive defense are mixed. There are people with whom I would like to develop relationships who will refuse to associate with me after reading Google information. I understand that their reaction is not unreasonable, but it hurts deeply.

In the void that arose from numerous rejections, I had ample time and reason to explore just what makes a story believable or unbelievable, and why it is so hard to combat and rectify fake news. In the following descriptions, I enthusiastically share what I discovered, for I believe the information has universal application. In a nutshell, I came to understand that human neurobiology adequately explains why "beliefs trump truth." There is a lot to this notion, which fills this book at various stages. I trust a reader will find it as fascinating and original as I find it relevant.

***

Once upon a time the study of psychology was the source of information used to explain human behavior. In the past, the human mind was viewed as separate from the brain. Biology, which determines psychology, could not provide tools with enough resolution to explain behavior on a mechanistic level. Then along came revolutionary technical advances in neuroscience, especially in brain imaging. With new tools, neuroscience began to explain psychology and the mind based on biology and biochemistry.

Mark Tramo, a neuroscientist at Harvard University in the late 2000s, inspired me and provided the insight that I needed to help understand why my true and verifiable account of fighting a corrupt legal system in Milwaukee did not register positively. After all, mine is a David and Goliath type story, and I was perplexed as to why it did not resonate as such. I continually wondered, *Why can fake news so readily prevail over the truth?*

Tramo had been investigating the odd—and today infamous—response to the first presentation of Igor Stravinsky's opera, *The Rite of Spring*, in Paris in 1913. He discovered that a group of specifically interacting cells in the brain, called the cortico-fugal network and located in the general area interior to the ears, monitors acoustic information that enters the brain through the ears.

The cortico-fugal cell network in the brain actually defines what a listener deems to be pleasant, unpleasant or intolerable sounds or music. Presumably, early memories from our developmental environment set these cells upon their judgmental and often permanent ways.

Behavior can be profoundly influenced by the cortico-fugal network, no less than by taking a drug, even causing radical behavior, thanks to its ability to produce unusually high levels of the neurotransmitter substance, dopamine. This explains the odd reactions of the opera-goers in Paris—staid, culturally elite and refined older individuals for the most part—as they broke into rioting when Stravinsky presented his bombastic, unusually rousing music at the venerated opera house.

In fact, the Paris opera-goers were led into a state of temporary insanity by the new, strange-sounding musical arrangement descending on them. Their reactions were caused by a mechanism similar to that of the mental illness known as schizophrenia. They revolted against the discomfort of the music by rioting just minutes after the performance began.

Not often thought of in this way, information can be a source of threat and pain—like fists, even as sound in the form of music.

So what does this information about an opera in Paris have to do with the believability of my strange story? A great deal.

A major discovery in the study of neuroscience and the brain is that the input of information (sound, sight, touch, smell) for each of our senses is processed in the exact same manner by the brain. The receptive sense organ does not determine the interpretation of the information that arrives to the brain. This characteristic of the highest level of the human brain, the cerebral cortex, is the result of what is referred to as the activity of the *common cortical algorithm*. This significant understanding is attributed to the neuroscientist Vernon Benjamin Mountcastle.

Based entirely on Mountcastle's discovery, I knew that what Tramo described for the processing of acoustic information for the sense of hearing must also apply throughout the brain for all of the other senses. This is not mere theory. For example, people have been taught to "see" by using sensations transmitted to their tongue after their normal sense of vision failed.

I reasoned that individual beliefs that we hold as true are an amalgamation of all of the human senses coupled to personal memories or experiences from the past. It was not much of a stretch of the imagination to see that, as with sound, there must also be groups of interacting cells at work throughout the brain to monitor and guard the sense of smell, touch, vision and even … beliefs. I use the word "guard" here in the sense that information too disturbing or outside preset limits leads to avoidance reactions or even violent reactions in response to ensuing discomfort. Most importantly, this guarding mechanism also governs our beliefs.

Why should something as simple as a difference of opinion (i.e. thoughts arising from word sounds) between people, for example, be so disturbing as to cause the end of deep friendships? Why can two contrary opinions lead to a physical fight, especially after drinking alcohol? What is the biological basis for the incredible power of beliefs—in essence encountering words or sounds molded in meaning by the past—to motivate extreme

71

behavior and all manner of seemingly irrational acts?

The emphasis and concern placed on what another human mind believes is reflected in the weight given to, for example, confessions. What is it about a confession that makes it so important? Of course, in a police/crime setting it is critical for practical reasons. Even so, confessions seem to have a power far beyond the merely practical. In the legal system, it is exceeding difficult to reverse a confession, even after it has been unequivocally demonstrated through physical evidence that the confession had to be false. Was the real crime by the accused a failure to adhere to a fixed system of beliefs, a demonstration of some sort of primal weakness on their part?

Recently, the Chinese government abducted and detained its own Beijing University students, students who had espoused what the government considered extreme Marxist ideology. Getting the students to see the wisdom of terminating their offensive activities, however, was not sufficient. All of the students had to prepare statements for public consumption, confessions confirming that their beliefs had been misguided. There had to be certainty that threatening beliefs, not only actions, were wiped out.

We are all aware of countless other occasions and venues whereby a person was required to confess to having believed in the wrong ideology, especially in wartime settings. Children are sometimes forced to verbally renounce behavior, vowing to replace it with other beliefs. Intuitively or at a subconscious level, we may have an understanding of what is at the heart of the power of beliefs. But the topic is too seldom discussed intellectually or seen rationally for its actual nature, the fundamental biology that underlies that power of beliefs and how that biology may determine who we are more than "we" determine who we are.

The answer to questions on the power of beliefs, I posit, lies in agitating a "belief cell network" akin to the cortico-fugal network. The way we respond to new information, that is our perception, has to do with how these belief cells have been trained by memory (or brainwashing) to select what is a "good" belief and what is a "bad" belief. Thus, we can feel discomfort when encountering a different belief.

There may be a compelling need to dominate or to reverse an encountered belief. Some discomforting beliefs are so threatening that they need to be permanently eradicated, as if they were a venomous animal capable of reappearing if not destroyed, and biting.

An observation made with baboons within their social network helps shed some light on the evaluation and impact of sound input to the brain. Audio recordings were made of baboons in social gatherings, at play, and in typical interactions. When these recordings were played back to the baboons through a loudspeaker, no attention was paid as the baboons went about their usual business. However, when the recordings were edited and scrambled so that baboons of lower social rank were heard raising their voices to baboons of higher rank in a challenging way, normal activities immediately stopped; all ears were raised in concentration.

Does truth have a sound? Yes, it does, and not infrequently a sound like the first few minutes of the *Rite of Spring* at its first performance for its first audience. A question should be asked: Can new information readily be seen as the truth if it causes discomfort?

Mention how, aside from direct pulmonary issues, cigarette smoke hardens arteries with every puff and watch the predictable reaction on a smoker's face. Better to push that information aside.

There is a solid, biological reason why truth can be unwelcome. Like a toothache, it can cause pain. To prove this point, research has shown that taking the common pain reliever, Tylenol, reduces the emotional discomfort of a breakup to a relationship. Not surprising at all, once it is understood that emotional discomfort can stimulate the same brain center as physical pain.

I recall years ago, working in what was then Rhodesia (Zimbabwe today). It was 1972. I was trying to explain to rural Ndebele tribesmen that the United States had placed a man on the moon. This information met with wide eyes at first, then grins shared amongst fellow listeners, followed by snickering and the admission of total disbelief directed at me as in "Aye, but no, man."

The cells that guarded the beliefs of the Ndebele tribesmen had had no exposure to any previous, surrounding or supporting information on this topic, as in the run-up of history, the space race with the Russians, etc. Their memories could not help explain this strange claim by an outsider. The information simply had to be nothing other than ridiculous.

***

Consider what it means to "believe" any telling of a story. In the absence of hard facts, believing an account that is heard is nothing but a personal judgment. There are two factors that determine what may safely be considered the truth: 1) personal memories influence and determine believability. Never heard of people being on the moon? The account of such is then not likely to be considered a true story; 2) the intrusion of fear due to the implications of a story being true.

The fact is, the human brain is cautious about what it wishes to believe because beliefs can be a matter of pain, or even life and death—like any physical threat. The "belief cell network," wherever it may be located in the brain, makes us aware of what we should dare to believe based on experiences and the associated memories that have helped us survive so far.

Regarding the story of my bizarre, frightening and unbelievable past in Milwaukee, I might as well have been telling the people whom I met that I also walked on the moon. It was simply unrealistic to think that anyone would believe me, the more so if I went into details. But worse than that, people thought that I was possibly an unstable confabulist for telling a true story.

Of course, no "belief cell network" can evaluate actual truth. It can merely determine what makes us uncomfortable about any story based on the listener's experience, just like the music heard in Paris. Personal memory will thus initially determine what a person does or does not dare to consider the truth when he or she hears a story.

In terms of important stories that we tell ourselves, religion surely tops the list. It is a crucial part of the "belief network" intrinsic to most human beings.

Unlike the USA, Switzerland does not feature any especially active, politically influential religious groups such as American Evangelicals. Secular and moderate go far in describing this country in terms of spiritual beliefs.

The Discover Switzerland (Presence Switzerland PRS) website is a good place to research various Swiss demographics, including the breakdown of language, traditions, cuisine, culture, and religion, among other facts.

Freedom of religion is a basic constitutional right in Switzerland. We are a primarily Christian country, with 36% of us being Roman Catholic, 30% protestant reformed and other, and 26% percent of the population being non-religious. About five percent are Muslim, and around 0.3 percent Jewish.

The second largest religious group here is comprised of mainstream Protestantism at just over 27%. The Swiss had their own version of Martin Luther, the father of the Protestant Reformation, in the form of Ulrich Zwingli. Zwingli, a contemporary of Luther, fought for religious change even before Luther did. Swiss Catholics had their own, deeply entrenched "belief network" at the time, which made it extremely difficult to question, let alone take a stand against abuses in the Catholic Church.

Today, the Swiss Roman Catholic Church, as in the United States, suffers from information that for too long was considered fake, but in fact was all too real.

As a former Catholic choirboy who was subjected to continual religious propaganda in my youth, I read of the seemingly endless cases of sexual molestation involving numerous victims of priestly abuse with astonishment. The success of the concealment of such gross conduct for so long can make sense, however. The momentum or inertia of the Church's powerful and official story, the story of the holy priest, has been among the most formidable in resilience and it offers a good example of how fake news (in this case promoting denial) can rule reality.

As an example, let us imagine that Archbishop Jones, who happens to be a close acquaintance, has been exposed by a friend for sexually abusing boys. Especially if you are Catholic, the consequences of believing this friend are likely to be frightening, profound, even life altering. You might consider having to leave the Church. In this regard, recent research on trauma is of relevance, showing how it can substantially influence memory.

The reality of any situation can pass an observer by and then be substituted by a less discomforting story, as the listener tries to make personal sense of incoming information based on his or her memories. For example, an eyewitness to a crime who has an inordinate fear of black crime may think that a crime that they witnessed was perpetrated by a black person when, in fact, that person was white. This need not be deliberate misrepresentation. The elements of the trauma that skew the perception and substitute reality with non-reality are shock and fear. They impact what a person truly believes they saw.

Now consider the sudden awareness that a close associate, the archbishop in this case, is a pedophile. There would surely be shock and fear as a reaction, and the same parts of the brain would interpret the information. That shock and fear can just as readily skew the story that we tell ourselves after the vile disclosure. A most common reaction would be that the disturbing report will initially be considered "fake." A "kill the messenger" response would be a legitimate response, based on normal brain biology.

Such responses must be considered normal, not an aberration, even if morally reprehensible. They arise naturally and help the listener deal with the arising stress. The substitute story that we tell ourselves can relieve the arising stress, like a pain killer. We can and should expect denial of a true story that challenges entrenched beliefs.

Der Spiegel, a highly regarded German magazine that

happens to have the world's most extensive fact checking infrastructure, recently fired its star reporter, Claas Relotius, after he admitted writing numerous, ostensibly true stories that were ... entirely false. Astonishingly, none of his stories had been fact checked. The reporter's portrayal of a heartless, blundering American society resonated well with a large segment of the German reading public. The stories Relotius wrote fit perfectly with reader belief systems.

Juan Moreno, the freelance reporter who helped expose the scandal, observed that, "One thing you can learn from reading pieces by Claas Relotius is that this is an easy world. It's easy to explain. It's easy to understand. And this is what Relotius really offers."

As I read about this incident in *The Atlantic* magazine, I was fascinated by the quote attributed to the reporter after he was caught. He informed his editor that, "I'm sick and I need to get help." This is the kind of confessional phrase one might expect from a pedophile priest, or a gambler with three children who had, once again, spent the family rent and food money. But a journalist referring to his own writing? At first it struck me as extreme, but in fact the perversion of truth or reality is a sort of sickness and it is dangerous, yet we have legions of writers today who pledge their allegiance to their, and our, easy beliefs, the beliefs that readers prefer. Of course, readers are complicit, like the German readers above, preferring that their stories reflect their beliefs, facts then being subordinate. If seeing facts means disrupting an entrenched belief system, then seeing may not be believing.

To be sure, meaningful accusations of wrongdoing can surface and have surfaced against powerful figures and institutions, e.g. the Catholic Church and renowned, respected medical doctors, major celebrities and football coaches. Equally, however, numerous people seem to have known about the abuses for years, and did nothing. What should we make of this?

For one, the concept of "if you see something, say something" applies best when a miscreant is a member of a lower social order. We see this repeatedly, when influential people in organizations get away with misconduct for years, sometime quite obviously. The concept of reporting to authorities can work too well when the source of supposed offense is e.g. of black color, or Muslim or poor or just socially insignificant. The story is easy in that case: people who enjoy little power can be bad people who do bad things. The baboons mentioned earlier can tell us something about stories that are harder to hear and believe.

Several reliable sources have estimated the percentage of abusive Catholic priests as in the area of six to eight percent. What about the other ninety-four percent? Surely some or even most of them should have known something was going on, in many cases over the course of years. Yet silence mostly prevailed, even extending to aggressive forms of denial that further harmed victims.

Should we refer to the silent ninety-four percent of priests, or a portion thereof, as evil? If we do so, we need to factor in that we should consider a large chunk of the human race evil, including perhaps ourselves. Few individuals have the courage to confront or contradict the prevailing story that powerful or handsome or successful or religious people must be virtuous. A new story needs to be created culturally. For example: "Priests, too, can be evil." But that takes time and exposure and persistence.

Any story heard by any individual is monitored by

neural cells in his or her brain, comparing it to their comforting, established beliefs. For example, inform devout religious people that you are an atheist and that you think they are misguided in their belief, and their "belief cells" will take adequate note of your words. Conversely, when a person of devout faith informs you that you are a misguided atheist in desperate need of redemption, your own "belief cells" will also take serious note.

We navigate a confounding cluster of political and religious dogma and cultural icons that ultimately determine what we consider good or bad, true or false. But we should be aware of and accept that truth can be subservient to beliefs, and perhaps must be so biologically, at least for a time.

Recently, the Washington Post reported that two young Americans on a bicycle tour of the world were deliberately run over by a motor vehicle in Tajikistan, and killed. The men who perpetrated the attack justified their act by explaining that the victims were "non-believers."

Was the attack senseless? We would like to think so as we express our outrage. But in fact, from a biological/neuroscience perspective, the incident is understandable and it does make sense … *if* there is full appreciation of the biochemical impact that such conflicts in beliefs—pure informational conflicts—can create in the brain.

Now, if we had heard that the bicyclists had threatened the killers physically beforehand, our reaction to the act would be quite different. But higher up in the brain, physical and psychological threats can merge and provide similar results, calling for action.

The ability of contrasting beliefs to transmute into physical reaction is a part of our normal makeup. Calling such a reaction a mental disturbance on the part of perpetrators only misses the point. What would be senseless is failing to understand the underlying biology that explains the behavior.

This is in no way an excuse for the murders. But here, exactly, is where conventional legal systems falter. If there is a biochemical explanation for behavior, and that biochemical reaction is autonomous, then how can a defendant be found guilty? Better to ignore the neuroscience. Too complicated. There is here, however, an explanation of why some may feel justified in committing such horrendous acts while the rest of us recoil at what we perceive as senseless and unthinkable.

When I challenged prominent lawyers in Milwaukee with accusations of their corruption, a story that reverberated with anxiety for both the media and the legal community there, the reach-back that made the most sense (and was the simplest) was one of psychiatric illness on the part of the storyteller (this author). Such a devastating accusation immediately alters the thrust of any story. It was thus used in my case. To aid this perception, the Milwaukee Journal Sentinel had published my picture in the paper, but not a recent, full cover page photo with me in a tie and white shirt as featured on a Wisconsin business magazine touting my business acumen, but a twenty-year-old photo from Africa, of me with a beard, looking like a beach bum. The story must fit the prevailing culture, not the truth.

***

The American legal system has been an area of my focus for the overall topic of truth versus the false story for many years. Nowhere else, perhaps, is the modification of truth into a false but easy story as prolific and significant as in the legal system (journalism being a possible exception). I offer the following for illustration of the point, many other examples being covered in my book *Lawyers Broken Bad* (www.lawyersbrokenbad.com).

The average person finds involvement with the legal system among the least pleasant, most anxiety-inducing experiences in life. Premature deaths and illness have been attributed to the stresses involved in legal disputes. Only lawyers enjoy legal match-ups, as they tend to win regardless of who loses.

The fear of the legal system has several consequences. Citizens who might provide exculpatory or incriminating evidence become shy, exhibiting avoidance behavior. Their "stories" can change remarkably, if the willingness to tell them at all does not entirely evaporate.

Next to clinical psychologists, criminal defense lawyers may be the group most versed in human behavior, or at least the specific human behavior exhibited under extreme pressure and fear. Lawyers quickly learn that, "Everyone is guilty of something" and involvement with the legal system can shake loose unpleasant memories. That can be advantageous in cases in which evidence and exposure are not welcome. The degree of fear of such a system leads directly to the ability to manipulate an official story.

At the same time, lawyers and prosecutors may be tempted by this common avoidance behavior on the part of ordinary citizens to engage in ethics violations and rule flaunting. They do not fear meaningful challenge to violations of fairness or even law by laity who themselves fear the system (just as Catholic priests felt protected by a powerful church and their positions therein), while resistance to poor conduct from within the legal system can be muted by interpersonal relationships—or "kompromat" (compromising material)—equivalent to the words "… by the way, do you remember when you needed help out of your jam, or that nasty situation with a friend's wife?" etc.

That elevated position, where a story told officially by the legal system takes precedence, has put considerable power in the hands of legal practitioners and has also led to great abuse in storytelling.

Recently, The Marshall Project (www.themarshallproject.org) reported the case of Corey Williams, a black, mentally disabled man found guilty of first-degree murder for a crime that he did not commit. (podcast at (https://www.wnycstudios.org/story/case-point-corey-williams). A false confession and concealed evidence led to his fate, but what catches the eye here is an odd reference to a *summation* of the case provided to the court by the prosecution. The summation *summarized* witness transcripts to state the polar opposite of the original, exculpatory transcripts. The summation was, in fact, pure fraud put forth by the prosecution. The actual transcripts, which would have exonerated Williams, were never presented to the court and thus not considered by the court.

The significance of this *summation* (i.e. telling a false story) as a major factor in the corrosion of justice cannot be overemphasized. Truth was thereby vanquished by a single submission of false evidence. William's true story fell into the hands of what was, in practice, his enemy. Innocence turned into guilt just through made-up words that fit an easy story about a black man. Note: this was done legally … no one objected until too late. Summations are an accepted part of the legal process.

The above violations of fairness took place in

Louisiana. The same circumstances—summations falsified with impunity—exist in the State of Wisconsin.

In Milwaukee, two court-ordered psychological reports were intentionally altered in *summations* to a federal judge. The summations to both reports stated the opposite of the originals. They implied that a father suffered serious mental illness in a case involving his son. The judge then ruled to prevent the man from seeing his son based on the false information. He also ordered that the man take his medication. But what medication had been ordered and by whom?

One false report submitted to the judge stated that the man "*refused to take his medication.*" Yet no medication had been ordered by any actual report or professional.

The psychologist who issued the original report was contacted for his reaction. When asked to refute the false report, he replied, "There's no need for me to do that; that summation is obviously false. I don't have the power to prescribe or order any drug be taken. Public record confirms that."

A psychologist is not a psychiatrist, a doctor with the power to prescribe medicine, a critical fact overlooked by the perpetrator of the summation fraud.

A court order later demanded that a third psychological report be carried out. The third psychologist carefully examined the two previous, original reports, concluding that a third report was a waste of her time. There were no problems to be identified with the man, neither earlier nor there in her office, and she informed the court of such after one interview. She also went on to question the discrepancy between the summations and the original reports.

The court took no action after receiving this information from the psychologist ordered by the court.

When the second psychologist was later notified of the fraud, he also accepted the fact that his original report had been altered.

"All right, all right," he admitted. "Other reports might also have been altered. But I'm close to my retirement; I'm not going to raise this issue now."

The Wisconsin Psychological Association received the relevant information and a complaint was sent to their ethics committee chairperson. In diabolical irony manifest as an incomprehensible lack of awareness, the response was as fine an example of psychological denial as can be found. Despite being presented with the false summations along with the authenticated original reports, the chairperson terminated the investigation. In an email he wrote, "What you describe simply cannot happen; it would be the height of mendacity for anyone to do such a thing."

In reply to this comment came "What about the documentation? The reports? Will you comment on the discrepancies?"

"I'm sorry," the psychologist wrote in conclusion, "there is nothing more that I can do for you."

This refusal to examine unequivocal evidence by a psychologist responsible for his organizations' ethics is one, small example of the power of the legal system to intimidate, to stop uncomfortable questioning, and to go with the story that "makes sense."

The subject of this story—the father—was actively prevented by the legal system from seeing or making contact with his son, including prohibition of written correspondence, from age five to eighteen.

But wait one minute! Even compared to many accounts of serious legal system wrongdoing, this case appears extreme. Why such a clearly cruel, excessively punitive response to a father? One explanation is that the father had been writing essays and booklets exposing legal system corruption in Milwaukee. Those writings involved a prominent lawyer and a judge. The written accusations had hit their mark. The response was to crush the criticism, eliminate the story and substitute it with fake news. What better way to clear an opponent off the shelf than to have accusations of mental illness sweep away his credibility?

After the false reports had been submitted, a lawyer who stood to benefit financially by protecting colleagues exposed by the father's essays contacted the father's lawyer.

"Your client is mentally ill," the lawyer pronounced in unconcealed triumph. There was thus no need for further effort in defense, he claimed. Another lawyer, who had supported the father in his pronouncement of Milwaukee lawyer misconduct through a letter that was made public, was hauled in front of a judge and warned that his career might be in play if he continued in that direction. And thus, the story the father had told of Milwaukee legal system corruption wafted into the thin air and disappeared, the claptrap of an ill man. A true story had just been replaced by a story that more people of influence felt comfortable with and that the public would readily accept.

When the rules are violated in the legal system—more so than elsewhere because elsewhere cannot imprison and destroy lives as readily—rapid moral degeneration can follow. The system can turn into a sadistic arena where, weakened ever more, a victim only whets the appetites of men attracted to a venue where other men must feel fear because of them.

***

A victim blamed for their own victimhood when telling a true story will surely be aided if they understand the explanatory concepts as presented in this book. An adverse reaction to a true story must be expected based on brain biology. The more entrenched a story is within a culture or a tribe, the more it can be considered to have its own momentum and the more difficult it will be to change the course of that story.

The negative reaction to disturbing information should be factored in by any storyteller in advance of telling a story. And indeed this is often the case, unfortunately, in the form of, "I thought no one would believe me so I remained silent." The agony of "Why won't anyone believe me?" becomes at least understandable through neuroscience, especially when the story involves threat to or by power structures.

It seems far more reasonable to attack the problem of silence in the face of wrongdoing from the point of view of understanding the problem. Bemoaning human weakness and demanding, as from the wilderness, that human nature change—that is, the way in which the brain processes information that challenges its beliefs—would seem to be futile.

After my explorations in this field, I am more aware intellectually now that a story has to fit the framework of the culture in which the story is being told. It has to fit the hierarchy. At an early stage of storytelling, truth and evidence may be dismissed or even despised.

When a story is a cultural mismatch, then careful consideration, planning and preparation need to occur in order to tell that story. The truth can prevail eventually, but there are solid biological reasons why it might be ruled out at first.

A reader may well say that the above, theoretical explanation is excessive, just a complicated way of saying what everybody already knows anyway. Of course, people know that stories must make sense within an environment of specific listeners. True stories are commonly modified to be acceptable in the context of who happens to be listening. False criminal confessions, for example, represent stories that come to please the interrogators based on their hierarchy and power.

Yet when an individual feels the sting of rejection for telling a true story, a deeper understanding of the neurobiological normalcy of *not* being believed can help to sustain that individual. It can lower their expectations at the start and lead to perseverance in telling a story where truth is less than welcome. If the expectation exists that a true story will be believed and it is then rejected, the danger exists that the storyteller will become despondent and lose the will to continue telling the truth.

This concept, of attributing causation, is well known in the medical profession in modified form. Once an ailment or a group of symptoms gains a medical diagnosis, the patient feels better and they can focus on conquering the illness. There is now something concrete at hand. This is what researcher Tramo's neuroscience information did for me. It helped remove me from the personal pain of my continual rejection. And to understand all, it is moreover said, is also to forgive all.

X. Unarmed and Harmless

"My rank is the highest known in Switzerland: I'm a free citizen."
~ George Bernard Shaw, Irish playwright and political
activist

One of the reasons why I refer to my record as an Airbnb Superhost is that I am disproving the false "armed and dangerous" etc. narrative pinned on me quite successfully by vengeful lawyers. A reason for publishing this book is defiance of those who wish to redefine my true history and end my storytelling. I have been at this rectification now for more than twenty years. I am a persistent, squeaky wheel that refuses to be silenced.

As a point of optimism, it should be mentioned that, after the initial outrage to, uproar about and rejection of the "strange, irritating sounds," Stravinsky's *Rite of Spring* went on to be accepted and even praised one year following the riot in the opera house. It counts today among the great musical masterworks. Persistence indeed pays off and must be employed against any lie. Biochemical processes in the brain start their work in disbeliever minds toward accepting the truth, but that requires time and repetition.

I first published the roots of the above concept of beliefs governing truth in the journal *European Neurology* in 2007, along with coauthor and Professor of Neurology Julien Bogousslavsky. As I have thought more about this phenomenon of brain cells "guarding" us from unwanted information, I also came to better understand two significant concepts associated with any "unbelievable" story on a neuroscience basis: "kill the messenger" and "blame the victim."

Both the reactions of "kill the messenger" bringing us bad news and "blame the victim" are simply a reflection of the fact that information can cause pain. After all, the brain determines what will cause pain and to what extent for any given individual, both physical and emotional pain. They are different sides of the same coin, meeting up at the same place in the brain but with a different sort of feel. Encountering a belief that disrupts an entrenched belief hurts. And just like physical hurt, we do what needs to be done to keep it away.

Education and evidence do eventually change minds toward the truth. But I found few people around me who had the time or wished to make the effort to verify what I told them about my past. Why should they? Switzerland is a hard rock of tradition and often-unquestioning respect for authority. The activities of a rebel are not welcome.

I also knew well in advance, given the above information, that my explanation to this extraordinary set of personal circumstances might not spare me from the torrent of fake internet news when I filled in the Airbnb host application. On the other hand, I had already been lucky beyond what could be expected on a number of occasions, when I slipped by one circumstance or another without Google information coming to bear. This included being hired by the University of Basel as a scientist and instructor, providing public science presentations. Soon enough, however, Milwaukee lawyers discovered what I was up to and made sure that the university knew they had hired a "dangerous criminal." But that is another story. In any case, history had taught me that the way things might seem to work isn't always how they really work. You have to keep trying.

***

I truthfully filled-in the Airbnb application for hosting, using my real name. I was approved as an Airbnb host within twenty-four hours. It did not take long until my first visitor arrived.

My apartment is a studio that I subdivided into two areas. There is no "studio apartment" category for Airbnb host accommodations in their location descriptions. I felt that listing my location as an "apartment" would mislead potential guests, possibly implying that I offered a separate, private room. This was not the case. I therefore classified my location downward one notch, into the "shared room" category. There would be visual privacy for a guest, but no audio privacy and no door to lock to the guest area.

I had a comfortable couch to sleep on when I had a guest, the guest had a bed even more comfortable. But I wondered, what kind of visitors could I expect for a "shared room" description? For example, would a woman book an accommodation listed as such with a strange male?

Yes to that. My first guest was an ultra-marathon runner from Chile, a twenty-five-year-old woman who arrived in Zermatt for the purpose of running an ultra-long but piecemeal lap around the Matterhorn. I was thrilled. She could not have been more pleasant, happy to share my space, and trusting.

My Chilean guest was working on her postgraduate degree in economics. I feel a special affinity to students—having taught at the University of Wisconsin, the

University of Basel as well as in Zululand, South Africa and for a short time in New Zealand. We had instant, warm rapport. But as I have practiced throughout with my guests, I didn't emphasize my real name.

Fake news portrayed me as something I was not. Fake news was the lie. It stripped me of true history and personal identity, replacing it with an "armed and dangerous" description that was intended to isolate me.

My guests come to Zermatt to enjoy the offerings of the village and Nature and to relax. I provide for their ability to do so beyond what they expect. Explaining my history makes no practical sense; it would merely frighten.

The location is described as "Martin's Eagle's Nest," in part to emphasize the outstanding view. My guests call me "Martin" and we leave it at that. The thrill of being in Zermatt and of carrying out their own plans overshadow any interest in me personally, with excellent reviews revealing their thoughts on their experiences.

To be clear, while guests are not made aware of my name, I do use it openly and everywhere else in town. Once in a while, a guest will hear someone call me by my name, but no one has ever questioned the disparity. Why should they? They are here to see Lovely Lady Matterhorn and partake in outdoor activities for a day or two. As long as they have a clean, affordable, safe place to stay and sleep and are treated with respect, they leave here happy. That is exactly how I and my guests like it.

The "Eagle's Nest" description isn't hyperbole. At 80 meters (250 feet) above the valley floor, the apartment windows and the balcony to the north face the Dom mountain. At 4,545 meters (14,900 feet), it's the highest mountain entirely within Switzerland, juxtaposed with the Täscherhorn, a spiked, canine tooth-shaped peak that appears higher than the Dom from my apartment, but really isn't.

To the south, and barely visible behind the Riffelalp hiking and ski area, rises the perennially snowcapped long, lazy arch of the Breithorn summit at 4,164 meters (13,660 feet), visible from my other balcony.

These are but three of forty-eight mountain peaks surrounding me, 4,000 m (13,000 ft) or higher here in the Canton of Valais. Of passing interest, the State of Colorado actually has more mountain peaks that rise above 4,000 meters (fifty-five), but they are not as dramatic and sharp-edged as the Swiss peaks. For one thing, they rise up from the Colorado Plateau, which is already one mile high.

The sun sets not on the horizon in Zermatt, but behind mountains that loom vertical, close and dark at the windowless rear of my apartment. But before it does so, it sets the Dom and the adjoining mountain chain aflame in a soft, orange evening glow. This can often happen as a guest and I are enjoying dinner. The view puts a pleasant and not uncommon end to my day, but a dramatic end to the day for someone from Seoul, Bangkok or Beijing.

Beijing? Those folks are happy just to be breathing our pure air. I even had a guest from Taipei, Taiwan, a young woman who claimed she had never seen stars before or even been in total darkness! She asked me if she might be allowed to keep her bed table lamp alight throughout the night. That starts one to thinking about human beings on Earth who are detached from the regular patterns of Nature. I felt sorry for her and agreed.

Miss Chile stayed with me for four days, a relatively long time as it would turn out. These days, my average stay is more like one or two nights. When she left, she gave me the first Airbnb review, five stars in each category I now recall, and some nice words. She received the same from me.

Another female guest arrived soon after the marathon runner, this time a tall, blonde German woman, middle aged, looking for a job at the old, fabled Kulm hotel on the Gornergrat, a 3,200 meter-high rocky ridge across the valley from the Matterhorn. One of Zermatt's most popular destinations, the Gornergrat overlooks the grand Gorner glacier, hosts a well-established astronomical observatory, and is the final stop in the ascent with our local, cogwheel mountain train.

The Swiss tourist industry and Switzerland in general are a haven for the relatively underpaid workers of the rest of Europe. Wages in Switzerland are considerably higher than anywhere else. So every once in a while I host people who are looking for a job here, just as this guest was doing.

The woman's stay with me was a one-day affair, and it almost turned into an affair in more ways than one. I brought her a cup of coffee in the morning, into her private space, while informing her that, "I'll be right back with some toast." On returning I was taken aback by the sight of my tall guest now completely nude, her backside prominent as she stood there, certainly not unattractively. What to do in such a circumstance?

It wasn't like me to pass up an obvious opportunity, but careful advance consideration of just such a situation and my role in hosting women warned me off. I felt privileged to be hosting people from all over the world. These people trusted me in a fundamental way. I had a responsibility to females for the trust they were giving me by entering my "shared room." Besides, and perhaps more importantly, this woman and I had not experienced any significant meeting of the minds. I placed the toast politely on the desk and headed back to the kitchen, not a word spoken.

Her review? Good except for cleanliness, which annoyed me. The place was clean. She claimed a vacuum cleaning would not have hurt. Not true and not fair. I had vacuumed and I do so after every guest.

"Leave it to an anally retentive German perfectionist," I muttered to myself as a form of comfort to my first critical review, "to make sure she found something to complain about." I was glad she had received no more than toast.

***

Over the course of time I have had to tighten up on some of the house rules for my guests. As previously mentioned, I had to start imposing restrictions so that people did not arrive after 7 p.m., to assure peaceful evenings and the preservation of private time. And I ask night owls—those who wish to stay out late—to book elsewhere. Showering and washing clothes after 9:30 p.m. are discouraged as well.

It mostly works out, as I tend to get the type of guest who is of the same mindset—active in daytime, sleepy in the evening. Take, for example, two Taiwanese—an outdoors program student and her sister, a music teacher. They visited just before this book was ready for publication, with nothing but Nature and the outdoors on their brains. They took the prize among all my guests for their intense desire to hike long distances in the mountains; they enjoyed my location so much that they stayed longer than initially intended, invited me along on two of their excursions, and radiated happiness the entire time. This was just the latest example of strangers who arrive, cheer me up and turn into friends. Upon leaving, they both left messages of appreciation written by hand on the chocolate box that they left as a gift. Each such kind act has imparted its sweet memory and collecting memories continues to be fun.

There are, of course, other online booking services that offer accommodations in Zermatt besides Airbnb. Couchsurfing is one of them. This matchup service between guests and willing hosts offers free accommodations, the finer points of who owes what to whom and for what being left to the parties involved to hammer out.

I never considered providing a Couchsurfing-type arrangement. I wanted the rules and my responsibilities clearly defined. In due course so far, I have had two guests who could not find Couchsurfing accommodations, and thus found their way to my place, one of the least expensive stays in Zermatt. Price-wise, I am just a bit above the local youth hostel.

One young lady who stayed with me explained the drawbacks of Couchsurfing this way: "It can basically become a dating service." On another occasion I had a male guest explain that he had slept his way through Europe using Couchsurfing accommodations—his latest stay being with a hairdresser in Zurich—but he was forced to book with me because he could not find a free place for the night in Zermatt. This was not an especially welcome piece of news. The next day, however, he did manage to find a willing partner, packed his things and violated his booking agreement with me. This was precisely the type of guest I did not wish to host.

***

There is no doubt, my apartment is close quarters. I provide the size of the private guest space in terms of square meters in the location description: six. Of course, a woman has the option of getting dressed in the bathroom if she chooses, with a door that closes. As of this writing, the percentage of my female guests averages about forty, these being overwhelmingly well satisfied with their stays.

For truth in advertising, I should say that the iconic Matterhorn peak cannot be viewed directly from my apartment. A walk of less than two minutes outside my door, however, does place her in view, and dramatically so. There she is, big and completely on her own on the skyline, as if no other mountain dared compete with her. She rests in stunning majesty, drawing tourists by the boatload from everywhere, faces aglow and in awe at first sighting her. There she is, as you round the corner outside my door and head downhill, the entire village spread out in front of you like a model railroad scene, for inspection, with the dominating church steeple centering the eye.

***

Back in July and August of 2015, my first year of hosting Airbnb guests, Zermatt celebrated the 150th anniversary of the first ascent of the Matterhorn. On July 14, 1865, Edward Whymper, Lord Francis Douglas, Charles Hudson, Douglas Hadow, Michel Croz, and two Zermatt guides, Peter Taugwalder and his same-named son made the historic climb. Not all made the descent back down. Croz, Hadow, Hudson, and Douglas perished. Whymper and the Swiss guides lived to tell about it. This story is now a central and oft-told part of local lore, and a major theme of our excellent museum.

As a part of the anniversary celebration, solar powered lights were placed by helicopter along the same route taken by the first climbers to scale the peak. As dark enveloped the village, the lights on the mountain were turned on for a wondrous, fifteen minute light show. That lasted for a few weeks, after which my guests went back to seeing the Lovely Lady on stage without the klieg lights.

Practically all of my visitors in the summer come here to see the Matterhorn and nothing else. In winter, some guests will say they come for the skiing or snowboarding, yet rare is it for one of them not to tell me proudly that they skied past her, or to complain about not seeing her due to clouds or fog. They would likely not be here without her.

The Matterhorn holds the town united in both pride and the financial advantage of having this attractive daughter pull in, in not a few cases, some very wealthy suitors.

The people who stay with me, of course, are hardly wealthy. A great many of them are students or recent graduates, or maybe just out of- or going into the army of South Korea. I am also used to hearing them tell me that they study IT, or computer programming, or are involved in business or marketing when they arrive. Lawyers I have had, one Korean medical doctor, also young, and several scientists. These people are usually on restricted budgets.

I did have a former major league baseball catcher, a Korean ocean freighter's first mate, a Swiss lake ship captain, a Harvard law student about to graduate who warned me not to vote for Bernie as Hilary was destiny, a Davidoff cigar representative and just one Russian.

Well that is not entirely correct. Before my first Russian male guest, I temporarily hosted a pleasant, young female Russian human resources officer who worked for a well-known social media company in Moscow. She was scheduled to stay with me for four nights, but that was truncated sharply by the abrupt appearance of two Albanians in her life. I never saw them or heard the details, as indeed I had no claim to such. All I really know is that she returned from visiting the Gornergrat area all a-gush, but not about the scenery.

"I met these two Albanian guys," she explained breathlessly in her heavy, Russian accent. "It's not that I don't like your place, not at all. But they invited me to stay with them in their hotel room. We are all heading back to Interlaken together tonight."

"Oh, their hotel room," I repeated with raised eyebrows.

Accompanying this explanation was the most devilish smile and body language that made it clear: she had the hots for these two guys, or maybe just for one of them but would tolerate the second. Brett Kavanaugh and the Supreme Court were still well in the future at that time, but the concept of the "devil's triangle" entered my mind nonetheless.

Raging hormones had likely given my guest the courage to leave a safe, secure abode and venture into a world far more exciting, if not possibly dangerous. This enthusiasm seemed to guide her somewhat sheepish but still joyful explanation, that she would be leaving my place early, in fact right there and then, but she did not intend to ask for a refund.

"I liked it here and I will give you a good review," she explained as she picked up her suitcase and headed to the door. She was true to her word and received my best review as well.

XI.   Goodbyes are the Hardest

"Switzerland is a country where very few things begin, but many things end."
~ F. Scott Fitzgerald, American fiction writer

I hadn't known anyone when I first arrived in Zermatt. Breaking into established circles anywhere in Switzerland is a tough act. Local talent is, of course, limited in many regards here anyway. It takes a certain mentality to remain in a village so small, so cut off from more diverse, urban culture, extensive amenities, and an extended horizon (literally). That mentality does not readily tilt toward the academic, intellectual or cultural side of things, while an interest in the outside doings of the world in general is also limited. That, after all, is the point of living in a small, relatively isolated village. So I often wind up engaging more with outsiders than with locals. This can be rewarding and interesting, but also too short lived, as those folks tend to leave.

As I mentioned previously, neighbors have asked me about my ease in letting total strangers stay with me. What I am doing is certainly not in line with typical Swiss norms, by which distance to outsiders is preferred. The fact is that many of my guests would have been invited to stay with me as personal, non-paying guests, the ambience was that good.

I often comment that, if my Airbnb guests are representative of the world at large, we have (or should have) a pretty good world. They bring enthusiasm and energy with them that rubs off on me. There is a caveat, however: most of my guests are also less than about thirty years old. Youth, in many cases, has not yet been ravaged by the vagaries of life, I conclude. They come open minded and share new insights and interests. My visitors, mostly eager learners and expressive, are a breath of fresh air in a country restrained in its emotional reactions to life or in shared observations with the outsider. The number of people I am glad to see depart constitutes perhaps ten percent of the total.

In contrast to the neighbor's question, I began to have somewhat of the opposite problem. After about three years of hosting Airbnb guests, I began to notice that saying goodbye constantly was unpleasant and tiring, even downright sad. This was a problem that I had not anticipated at the start. Guessing now at what may end my hosting, I doubt that it will be weariness of welcoming guests, but maybe becoming worn down by repeat departures. Saying hello is easy and fun, but saying good-bye, especially when you like someone, is hard work.

Nevertheless, there are times when good-bye is welcome. Aside from the guest who was still reliving his Swiss Army experience, the most perplexing, conflicting and upsetting encounter of my hosting career occurred just after I had successfully welcomed more than four hundred guests.

A Hong Kong Chinese woman arrived, forty years of age she willing informed me, full of enthusiasm and smiles. I knew immediately that Lynn would make her stay enjoyable for both of us.

Lynn was an obstetrics nurse in one of Hong Kong's largest hospitals, also a midwife and on her first vacation to Switzerland. We spent a few hours pleasantly talking about her experiences at her hospital in and I happily apprised her of my earlier years of setting up pathology clinics at two South African hospitals.

Lynn was not an official Airbnb guest on that day; she had asked me several days previous if I could accommodate her one day earlier than her booking. She had seen that another guest had booked her intended earlier date and explained that a mattress on the floor would do. I agreed. At the same time, my Airbnb guest that evening was to be a man from Seoul, South Korea. He arrived several hours after Lynn.

My initial impression of Ji was not ideal. He had failed to read the meeting instructions that I had specifically sent him. Instead of the appointed, easy-to-find meeting location, he arrived at dark on the lower level of my building, confused as to where to go, bothering my neighbors as he sought my apartment. His next misstep was to use my personal towel in the bathroom rather than ask for another.

Ji's two initial missteps, however, were mitigated by his openly pleasant personality and relaxed, easy-going manner. He reminded me of a middle-aged hippy, with hair in a ponytail, talk of his guitar playing, a consciously relaxed manner and an interest in the modification of raw reality through the use of various substances—never mind that I had never seen a South Korean hippy or anything close to that.

Ji and Lynn chatted amiably throughout the evening as he asked her to help him book his next stay in Switzerland, for his German language ability was non-existent and his English particularly poor.

It is clear from my location description and communications with booked guests well in advance that I require lights-out and quiet time at 10:45 p.m. All seemed well as Lynn settled in on a floor mattress on my side of the apartment, while Ji headed to bed on his side. But just after 11 p.m. I heard light tapping noises coming from Ji's side, along with a low level of light. Then I heard whispering. Upon inspection, I saw the two of them sitting on Ji's bed, gazing at a phone screen and, I guessed, playing a video game. I reminded both of them that I had to get to sleep, and Lynn headed back to her side of the apartment. It occurred to me that Ji, as part of his relaxed attitude, had either not read my entreaties regarding sleep, or simply decided to ignore them.

Either way, I was annoyed. I suspected that Ji had messaged Lynn in bed, perhaps asking her for more help with some internet issue, as he had been doing earlier, and she had responded, also oblivious to the house rule. Then things had evolved into game playing.

In the morning, at about 6 a.m. and while it was still dark, I heard Lynn rise from her mattress, to go to the bathroom I had assumed. I waited for her to return for my use of that facility when I realized that she had not gone to the bathroom, but instead snuggled under the covers with Ji in active coupling!

I sat up in bed, considering my options, as I had highly conflicting thoughts rapidly running through my head. I was certainly no prude. There was nothing wrong with two people engaging in sexual activity, but right under my nose in close quarters? I asked myself, *Would I engage in such activity with a woman while a guest was staying with me, and there was no opportunity for privacy?* The answer was unequivocally "No." Reason? A show of respect for another person, my guest.

I had the option of remaining silent or reacting. I waited until Lynn returned and then I blew my stack.

"What's going on?" I asked.

She looked sheepish, no answer.

I then approached Ji and said, "It's a matter of respect for me. You didn't bother to concern yourself with my lights-out policy, and you had no concern for me when you had her in your bed. Now, I want you to leave."

Ji began to smile, then attempted to put his arms around me for a hug, smiling, and not aggressive at all. I protested and resisted his attempts.

"You have to leave," I repeated.

And he did.

I then asked Lynn whether she was staying. She nodded. I was surprised. She was certainly half responsible for this incident, or even more so, but she had not annoyed me as Ji had. I did not mind her staying. But it occurred to me that I was far harsher on him than on her.

I felt morose that entire day and agonized over whether I had overreacted. I know that residences in Hong Kong are among the smallest and most expensive in the world. Perhaps expensive, confined spaces require greater tolerance. I had also read that such conduct is not unusual in Russian apartments. Do people elsewhere think differently about such things?

The concept of privacy, it is said, is only six hundred years old. Human sperm feature highly sophisticated defense mechanisms, mechanisms to attack other sperm from various sources. Sperm can only attack other sperm if they are on the same battlefield at the same time. Nature obviously knew our secrets.

Kim Tallbear, a professor at the University of Alberta who studies indigenous peoples, contends that before white settlers arrived, sexual activity took place among friends and in the presence of relatives as part of normal activities. I had also seen the movie *Black Robe*, with the "savages" making love in a communal area, quite naturally. Had I indeed still not been able to shake off my inhibiting Catholic education, where all things sexual needed be associated with shame or discomfort, even now as an atheist? But I kept coming back to my original reasoning: *if I had done that with a guest present, I would have felt like a pig, oblivious of someone else's feelings when they could not escape.*

That was the point: no escape. If the two of them had been secretly whispering about eating chocolate cake without me, I might also have been upset. I wasn't a potted plant. Just because I was the host, could I not expect the same courtesy that I extend to my guests?

Lynn returned from exploring Zermatt at the end of the day. She was friendly and attempted to converse naturally. It was I who had little to say.

The issue never came up again. She stayed two further days, pleasantly, and I began to loosen up. She had, indeed, been a fine guest otherwise.

When Lynn entered the elevator on her way back to Hong Kong, I suggested, "Best there be no review," and smiled. I am fairly sure I saw great relief in her facial expression. I just regret the incident entirely. One thing was certain: I would never have put any aspect of it on the internet in an Airbnb review.

To this day I am not convinced that my reaction was the best.

While on the subject, one noticeable absence from the commercial scene in Zermatt is the sex trade, yet debauchery in forms outlawed and restricted in many countries flourishes here in Switzerland. Zurich has numerous sex clubs frequented by businessmen from all over the world and serviced by providers often from Eastern Europe, Russia or Germany. Organized, publicized orgies are as common in Zurich as chocolate shops (almost). Of course, these establishments operate at Swiss standards of cleanliness, orderliness, and fiscal responsibility, all seemingly aboveboard and lawful.

Interlaken, for example, has its industrially zoned bordello, as do many villages. Zurich even erected prefab, container-like structures in its red-light district, for the ultimate in romance and privacy. But not Zermatt.

In general, the Canton of Valais is Catholic and conservative. I have never seen or heard of a sporting woman ply her trade here, outside or in, though surely it occurs.

Sex near the Matterhorn would have to be arranged privately, in hotels for example, and relying most likely on escorts traveling here from out of town. An old friend told me that, in years past, morally-inclined hotel owners even asked to see passports and marital status before allowing the rental of rooms. Those days, however, are long gone.

Of more than five hundred guests, I have only had one ask me a question related to acquiring sexual services in Zermatt. A gay gentleman from India asked, "Are there any bathhouses in town?" At first I thought he might be referring to the many wellness spas at most of the hotels, but no, he meant San Francisco style gay bathhouses.

"Geez, I have actually never had that question asked," I explained with a chuckle. "I doubt it; Zermatt is a place people come to for outdoor activities, not so much backdoor activities."

My guest was not amused.

Still, both romantic amour and plain, lustful sex are no strangers to my guests.

South Koreans, numbering most of my visitors, are especially artful in finding companionship when they arrive in Zermatt. They use a popular Korean travelers' app that leads them to equally lonely hearts drifting around the mountains here and, compared to other nationalities, they seem particularly well organized interpersonally through the internet. To my great pleasure, I have been told that my location is mentioned and favored on a main Korean travel site.

Alcohol also tends to flow liberally with my Korean guests, and it's no surprise that the Koreans are called the "Irish of Asia." Abandoned, unopened bottles of clear, colorless, ubiquitous soju, the Korean vodka, face me as I write this paragraph, among the various items and gifts left behind.

Some time ago I hosted a male Korean schoolteacher who, by chance, met a female Korean teacher using his traveler's app. He invited her to Sunnegga, one of three main vantage points reached by mobile means of ascent to view the Matterhorn, in this case by a four-minute funicular ride through a tunnel up to the top of the mountain.

Two bottles of wine were consumed on this particular excursion, followed by a request by the two of them to eat dinner with me at my place that night. Another two bottles of wine followed, together with a merger of the three of us into singing and swaying to Korean songs in our seats. At the end of the evening my guest escorted his catch back to her hotel and decided to spend the night there, presumably to protect her from dangerous Swiss influences. He returned next morning, well sated and happy.

The appeal of sharing this type of contentment and the joy that flows from guests at being under the Matterhorn is the reason why I continue to do Airbnb hosting. These two Koreans were just one more example.

This might not be the case if I were—say—hosting in Gary, Indiana, but people who visit me tend to be happy on arrival, and that is good enough for me.

XII.   Law and Order

"It's lawmakers know better than anyone that laws are more a matter of practical compromise than any kind of moral imperative."
~ Kim Stanley Robinson, <u>Antarctica</u>

L aw enforcement in Zermatt is discrete and, for the most part, invisible. Switzerland is vastly different from the USA in its policing practices. If society here is low-key, that goes double for the police. From time to time, two police officers may be seen walking purposefully along the main street here, or wheeling their narrow electric vehicle around town. They are present in the accurately perceived sense of safeguarding, protecting, being helpful, and they are not a particular threat to anyone of lawful intent. I found this to be the case all throughout Switzerland.

Interlaken, for example, holds an annual rock festival, a trucker festival and other large gatherings that attract youths and alcohol at a former military airfield. Attendance can vary anywhere from 5,000 to 35,000. These festivals include weekend, overnight camping. In eleven years of attending and observing those activities, I cannot remember seeing the presence of a single police car or even police! I found this astounding. No doubt critical information must have been exchanged undercover and appropriate actions undertaken, but quietly. Ostentatious displays of anything are not the Swiss way.

I once attended an outdoor theater presentation, at a

lakefront village not far from Interlaken. There must have been over one thousand locals in attendance, including young children, sitting in bleachers set up especially for the occasion. During the three-hour production there were simply no disruptions outside of intermissions, which were also very orderly. Focused attention, calm and quiet, prevailed. The level of attention to the performance and the respect for the performers and fellow audience members was extraordinary for an American to behold. That is vintage Swiss.

There is a darker side to this regimentation and respect for orderliness, of course. The individual is of lessor importance than the perceived good of all, even to the extent that infractions of law, ethics or theoretical rules will be tolerated if done at the top. This "discretion" may at times be beneficial practically and may seem to make some sense in certain cases, until it goes awry. The local mayor caught with his hand in the till or his hand down someone else's pants? That may well be handled quietly, internally. A victim may have to suck it up. Small changes in hierarchy will be permitted, revolutions to serve justice for the individual, maybe not so much.

*****

There are interesting statistics on levels of false confessions made to police in various nations. The last time I checked, the USA was considered to be at around thirty percent, Japan at an astonishing seventy percent. My guess is that Switzerland, for which I found no statistics, is closer to Japan than to the USA. In fact, there is such regard for hierarchy and the legal establishment in Switzerland—and fear of being the one to show the system short of perfection—that I have witnessed judges in courtroom trials bold enough to openly accuse a defendant of a crime with which they were never charged nor ready to defend, and the defense lawyer will stand by, quietly!

A friend who has lived in Zermatt for half a century reacted to my observation on Swiss policing and law enforcement by explaining that Zermatt, in fact, experiences the same categories of crimes as anywhere else, but fewer of them due to its size, of course.

Crimes and statistics on crimes are not advertised here, and there is a fundamental attempt to keep them from becoming crimes in the first place. Such statistics are of no commercial advantage.

The extent to which crimes happen is not always publicized as it might be in the USA, certainly not on local television news channels (because there are no local television news channels), and the police are sworn to confidentiality on individual matters. Obviously, local media have no great interest in emphasizing crimes that occur in a tourist destination. Discretion is also a characteristic of news reporting in this small country.

In Zermatt, I have never personally heard of a theft, not even of a bicycle, except for two instances of what appeared to be planned heists at top-brand watch boutiques. The loot apparently exceeded one million dollars in each case and took the mundane nature of a window and an entryway smashed through in the early morning hours. When incidents such as these do occur, the general consensus is that obviously outsiders, not Swiss, must have been responsible. Indeed, this often holds true. This is a common refrain throughout Switzerland. Tourists are welcomed, but foreigners bring trouble and crime.

I have often left my front door unlocked. Personal

safety in any regard is of little concern to me here. I have also never seen any instance of violence or public disturbance of any kind in four years here, and including the previous eleven years as well. That being said, I tend not to hang around urban areas. Outdoor folks are likely to have agendas apart from criminal activities.

My worst encounter in Zermatt has been with a neighbor who took an intense dislike to my feeding the birds.

"An unhygienic and filthy habit," my neighbor declared.

True, the birds would perch on the neighbor's balcony as they eagerly awaited my generosity. This, I admit, did lead to the release of previously metabolized nutrients on their railings and balcony table, highly likely also due to my generosity. But filthy and unhygienic? Compared to what, exactly?

As evident and observed with much appreciation by everyone who visits here, Switzerland is an ultra-clean country—on the surface, anyway. Cigarette smoking, inarguably among the filthiest of all habits in many important respects, flourishes here and is well tolerated. Butts, which persist interminably and are ineffective anyway, are tossed where you will.

About thirty-eight percent of the population smoke tobacco. Children are routinely exposed to smoke (with its 7,000 chemical constituents) as it wafts generously in public, outdoor venues—a throwback, as if medical information on the topic were not available.

Do not try to tell the Swiss (or the French) that smoking is bad; they will inform you that you are just another American obsessed with health concerns.

In clean Switzerland, male sperm counts have been dropping, while asthma and allergy rates are rising, as in many other western nations. At the moment, our local district attorney is hauling a major chemical company into court not far from Zermatt, for dumping carcinogens that can make their way into our hopefully clean mountain waters.

The following story illustrates a different Switzerland, one that tourists do not see and have no great reason to care about.

A Swiss plastics manufacturer in an industrial park near the City of Basel was emitting smelly exhaust from one of its manufacturing processes. An employee at a neighboring company identified the emissions as carcinogenic volatile organic compounds (VOCs). When questioned about their involvement the emitting company simply lied, claiming there were no such emissions. The employee then contacted the Swiss equivalent of the Environmental Protection Agency. They sent along a sniffer vehicle and verified the danger of the emissions, forcing the company to upgrade its installations.

The owner of the emitting company called the whistleblowing employee's boss, the company CEO, and complained about the exposure. The snitching employee was immediately fired, as the CEO informed him that, "This is not how we do things in Switzerland."

This story illustrates several points. There is theoretical law in Switzerland, and then there is tribal law. The CEO remarked that a violation of law should have been reported to him, first. This was obvious nonsense, merely an attempt to control at a private level that which is of public interest, for private benefit.

The owner of the company emitting the VOCs eventually called the whistleblowing employee himself and further complained, "You know, we are in an industrial park, not in the mountains."

In other words, poorer workers and their children living nearby had no need to be factored into the larger picture of clean Switzerland.

The remark, "This is not how we do things in Switzerland" by the employee's CEO also contained broad truth that resonates nationwide. In Switzerland, the prime anxiety and neurosis revolves around employment and unemployment. Jobs are the sacred cow to the point where companies can violate laws, as shown in this case, and workers can be trusted by convention to just keep quiet. That is the Swiss way. Discretion. "Keep your mouth shut; it isn't your business."

The image of Switzerland belies what can and does happen under the surface.

We are expected to be neutral here, whereby neutral automatically means favoring the status quo. This is true in an environment of generous unemployment compensation and a well-structured, efficient social net that includes universally good health insurance even if you are not employed. This security, however, does not ameliorate an underlying fear.

It cannot be doubted, the owners and employees of both companies in the above story put the highest stock in their being "clean" in the traditional, superficial sense. Immaculate offices, spotless factory floors, excellent personal hygiene. Make it all look good to the outside. Surface clean is part of the identity of the Swiss. Rocking a boat to reveal the rot underneath is not.

In conclusion to the above story, the employee took his employer to court for contract violation and improper dismissal. He won the case with no resistance from the CEO or the company. The judge did an excellent job.

Most Swiss will tell you that what the company did was wrong, and that the court decision was just what they expect. The typical Swiss mentality, however, makes exposing or challenging corporate or institutional wrongdoing uncommon.

The Swiss legal system can work, but it can also fail miserably in a very un-Swiss way, in violation of concern for quality or rule-following when a major institution is involved. Just as in the United States, legal due process can be trampled, clients betrayed by their own lawyers, and thus political needs become the victor over rule of law. This was the case, for example, at a Swiss university, where defense lawyers, betraying their own client, concealed exculpatory evidence pertaining to administrative failure and scientific wrongdoing, thereby protecting the reputation of the institution at the expense of the individual and scientific integrity.

Such illegal, unethical conduct can meet with a shrug from the Swiss, who turn passive when authority needs to be questioned or confronted. Rebels are weeded out at an early age here. The simple fact is, who wants to stand out as a lone soldier for truth and do damage to an institution when you need to keep functioning in a confined world? In this regard Switzerland is vastly different from the expansive, practically limitless opportunities available in a larger country, like the United States. The problem here is that the equation that describes the balance between cost and reward in such cases—institution versus the individual—can show that the cost associated with justice for the individual is too high to the group, making the diminishment of the individual troublemaker/whistleblower too tempting.

An article in the *The New Yorker* magazine on an allied subject happened to draw my attention. The article, *A Theory of Trump Kompromat*, contained a description that paralleled my experiences with the American legal system as well as the Swiss. A professor of politics at University College London and an expert on Russia's political practices, Alena Ledeneva, explained how power politics work in Russia. But there is no need to limit the general framework of her description to Russia.

The thrust of Ledeneva's description is the claim that power is distributed through networks of influential Russian individuals who follow unspoken rules within an informal hierarchy and outside of the law. Ledeneva calls the framework for this informal means of interacting the *sistema*, or system in English.

The *sistema* has certain rules that are never to be violated, but they are not the theoretical rules of expected social conduct or law. These rules are ambiguous and flexible, except for the priority that is clearly understood, and that defines the *sistema* and is its central feature: no one within the *sistema* should feel threatened by anyone else within the *sistema*. A delicate, intra-system equilibrium thus exists, effectively kept intact by the mutual threat of having and potentially using compromising information (in Russian, *kompromat*).

Each person in the *sistema*, Ledenova explains, continually questions where they stand and monitors the relative positions of friends and rivals.

In the legal system of Switzerland, *kompromat* can surely play a role, but perhaps the biggest role is played by an implied but diffuse career threat should, for example, a lawyer defend his client too vigorously to the detriment of a powerful institution or a fellow member of the legal *sistema*. The professional group will take note; opportunities dry up in a small country.

It would be a mistake to think that such a system works only in what we think of traditionally as corrupt countries. There is concrete evidence that segments of the legal systems of both Switzerland and the USA operate in this fashion; that is, lawyers acting outside the law to protect entrenched powers. It can even be argued that Switzerland, due to its small size and the "everybody knows everybody else" mentality here, is particularly vulnerable to this type of corruption.

The fact that the Swiss trust their institutions (or fear criticizing them and being accused of doing national damage) only provides an even more favorable playground for those with nefarious intent.

As it is, the Swiss are already too aware of their small national stature. Threat to one of their institutions that provides prestige and international reward and recognition in a competitive world justifies bending the rules. Unlike cheese and chocolates, the "quality" label is not necessarily affixed to Swiss legal products.

For tourists, however, all of this is entirely irrelevant; what could there possibly be to not like here in Switzerland? They love Switzerland in general and Zermatt in particular, each and every one of them, no exceptions so far that I have heard of (except for the common complaint about prices being high and, oh yes, lack of ski-lift seat heating).

Tourists value the short-term aspects—scenery, activities, accommodations, safety. At these Switzerland succeeds brilliantly. Visitors universally love Switzerland for many good reasons, not least the reliability of always on time public transport and the remarkable cleanliness, as if it related to goodness. Safe, reliable, clean and well organized sums up tourist Switzerland.

There is enough time for dinner and the dance party, but too short a time to go spying into the medicine chest or the closets.

XIII. Bill Cosby Gets to My Guest

"All generalizations are false, including this one."
~ Mark Twain

What could dozens of Chinese visitors to my home in Zermatt tell me about 1.4 billion Chinese whom I have never met? Maybe very little, but perhaps something useful and valid. But how to distinguish signal from noise in terms of relevance when a generalization is made? My conclusion is that my experiences with various cultures and countries of origin guide me, but I need to be careful; I remind myself to keep expectations within bounds. I hold back on assumptions about any individual who intends to visit me until I experience their presence.

Nevertheless, I cannot deny the autonomous feelings of expectations, negative or positive, that arise when I receive the "Congratulations" SMS message on my phone, indicating that another guest has booked my location through Airbnb.

The first thing that I do when a new guest has booked is to check gender, then the nationality. I look at the pictures; I get a good feeling if there are smiles. But why should I feel positive anticipation, for example, when a Japanese, Korean or Chinese woman books, as opposed to wariness when an American woman does? The following story helps explain this.

A twenty-six-year-old female, a Montana native and manager of a ski resort in the States arrived as my guest on a particular day when two stories were prominent in the news. My computer screen was abuzz with reporting about the Bill Cosby molestation fiasco, as well as an account of a woman who had successfully sued an oil company because she found a camera implanted in her private quarters on an oceanic oil-drilling platform.

My guest and I discussed these two stories for about fifteen minutes. I reassured her that Switzerland had a deserved reputation as a safe country for her travels in such matters and in others. The rest of the evening was uneventful. The next morning I escorted her to a nearby trailhead, pointed her in the direction of her desired hike, no issues apparent as I left her and returned home. When she returned in late afternoon, she abruptly declined a cup of tea that I offered. Five minutes later her bags were packed. She was heading out the door.

"I'm leaving; you frighten me," she explained when I asked what she was doing.

This thunderclap from a clear sky put me in a state of shock. Confused and deeply concerned, I asked, "But why?"

"You talked about Bill Cosby," she explained. And gone she was.

Five minutes later, two polite (they are all polite) Swiss policemen knocked at my door, demanding to know what I had done to my guest.

"Nothing," I said, still in shock. "I didn't do anything."

"What reason did she give you for leaving when she left?" one of the officers asked.

"That I frightened her ... because I spoke about ... Bill Cosby."

The officer grinned knowingly, looked at his partner and said, "Yes, that is what she also told us."

After some further explanation, I asked, "Is this incident going on record anywhere?"

"No," the officer assured me. "I'm not even entering it in my notebook. We have this kind of trouble with North American women. Obviously, she has had a traumatic experience in her past."

It seemed that I would not be alone in Zermatt in creating a generalizing category known as "North American women." The officer must surely have had the "past trauma" part right. Although it was an unjustified overreaction by my guest from my vantage point, I readily comprehended that its origin must have come from a frightening ordeal at some earlier time. While I was fully prepared to leave a review in self-defense to any accusation, I discovered that she had contacted Airbnb, cancelled her reservation and claimed that she had not spent the first night at my location.

I breathed a sigh of relief. Explaining the situation in a review would have been a nightmare. The result was that neither of us wrote a review. Later, I coincidentally discovered a fact that tied Bill Cosby, albeit loosely, to Switzerland. His private plane, a Pilatus PC12 turboprop, is manufactured by Pilatus Aircraft of Stans, Switzerland. Should my guest have avoided Switzerland altogether for that reason?

I was put on sharp notice by that experience. It clearly resonated in my future in terms of prediction. Supported by reality or statistics ... or not, I was generalizing about this emotionally charged event, and that aspect—the emotions—is the key to the reflex to generalize.

Such a confrontation, I have been assured by Asian guests, would not have occurred with an Asian woman. The Zermatt police had no "Asian women" category. As to why this is so, and whether it reflects anything other than suppression, fear, or the sensed futility of complaining on the part of women from Asian cultures, I cannot say. I can say that my guard to such a thing happening again is never raised when an Asian woman books with me.

By chance, sometime after my encounter with the North American category for women, I ran into another instance of the North American category of generalization emerging here. A local expert on skiing in the area remarked that, "If there is trouble skiing off-piste, you can be sure it will be due to some North American, some cowboy."

I took note of this remark and added it to my list of generalizations, and how and why they arise, as I will discuss here a bit later.

***

While by far most of my guests can be said to have traveled to Zermatt for the pure pleasure of travel itself and viewing Nature, not everyone who visits my home here arrives happy, unfortunately. I have also had my share of escapees from wounds following personal losses in life.

To date, there have been a total of two encounters with female guests that ended unpleasantly, the second unrelated to Bill Cosby or North America in any way, but due to an expression of my opinion.

An Australian woman, twenty-two years of age, stayed with me for four days, peacefully and pleasantly. Her visit, however, had not been without an unusual aspect at the start. Within ten minutes of arrival, she unburdened herself by telling me that she had had an abortion and had never told anyone else about it. She was first generation Australian of Chinese extraction, she explained. She didn't want her parents to know about the abortion.

It was unfortunate that an Airbnb host and stranger had to be her outlet for this obviously personally painful information. I listened attentively and sympathetically. But on her final morning while eating breakfast, something happened that was just as puzzling as the incident with the woman from Montana. I expressed my opinion about a certain religious faith, one underpinned by a philosophy that had acquired a reputation for intolerance toward female independence, and I began to provide examples of this. Suddenly, again out of the blue, she burst into tears, became angry and accused me of being prejudiced and a bigot. Had her boyfriend been of that faith? I had no clue.

The unexpected, intense display of emotion was surely frightening. Irrationally, I was prepared for another knock at the door after she left, which, of course, never came. There was no review of the stay in either direction.

Conversations with guests can lead anywhere. However, if I sense that a guest has political or philosophical leanings other than mine, I try to remember that I have an obligation to be a cordial host. I refrain from engaging in arguments. After all, my guests are more or less trapped here with me. My goal is to have a happy guest, and if that isn't my goal I should not be a host.

As I have been in the Airbnb Superhost category through guest appraisals and reviews for, currently, nine straight quarters, by far most people like my hosting style. I work hard to maintain this status.

Earlier on in my hosting I was hovering at the margins of the Superhost category, until I began explicitly warning would-be guests that my location is up a steep hill (as posted in the location description). I also now routinely ask guests, while they are here, whether my standards of cleanliness are adequate. Could I improve on anything? No one ever complains and my cleaning habits have not changed. But merely asking the question on cleanliness has worked wonders. These two categories had been my weakest; when they improved, I was able to enter the Superhost category regularly.

Even with all of my clever ploys to achieve guest satisfaction, criticisms can pop up when least expected. For example, I handed a guest from the Middle East, who seemed well pleased with his stay, one of those super-absorbent microfiber travel towels, soft and large but thin, without giving it the slightest thought. In his review, he accused me of giving him a "tissue" to dry himself. Because of that comment, I now offer guests a choice, old-fashioned towel or high-tech "tissue."

The same guest found fault with the hand soap in the bathroom. "Unhygienic" he complained. Actually, the bathroom had both, hand soap and a liquid soap dispenser. His claim of hand soap being unhygienic, however, is groundless nonsense. Younger folks are apparently not aware that there was a time when, somehow, the world survived without liquid soap.

***

Refugees from failed relationships and other sorts of problems can wind up in a place like Zermatt, too. While upbeat spirits and joyful appreciation of Nature among my guests far exceed their opposite, I have had memorable visitors who were suffering from loneliness and rejection. Some of that suffering, which I could not help but feel myself in close quarters, came from the disappointment that arises from realizing at a profound level that, for example, ultra-heavy bodies invite attention and attraction less than my guests desired.

The majority of overweight guests visiting me have been North American; rarely Asian. These few guests spent their time on the phone or watching movies and eating. It was heartbreaking. The draw of a blue sky, soft southerly breezes and snowcapped peaks did not prevail over ruminating in isolation during their days. I am a willing listener in such cases. Yet it is sad; no matter what political correctness and courtesy dictate regarding the avoidance of body shaming, I have witnessed destructive body shaming that comes from inside the person themselves.

Unlikely as it might seem given the venue, some of my guests here in Zermatt are struggling with or escaping from drug addictions. These folks would never be Asian, I now make the assumption, but American, yes.

I hosted two guests in close order, American men who had both inherited large sums of money, one from an asbestos insurance settlement earned by his father, the other an inheritance upon the death of a father. Both had been in rehab for addictions and neither had reached twenty-four years of age. Drugs were a part of their lives.

While smelling it wafting in the air anywhere in Switzerland is not unusual, even marijuana is illegal here. Being caught with less than 10 grams can trigger a fine, while over that amount is courting a criminal problem.

I do not allow smoking of cigarettes or otherwise, not even on my balconies. To my knowledge, no one has ever used illegal drugs in my apartment, and only one Californian asked to be allowed to smoke marijuana. Talk of drug use or reference to such by my Asian guests remains unheard of.

Neither of these two American guests had done their research on Zermatt. They were unaware that we have a prohibition on automobiles in the village. There are special, narrow-bodied electric taxis that buzz around, but cars are not allowed. In fact, since its beginning Zermatt has never allowed private cars to drive into town. Indeed, there are no roads for normal-size cars for a good part of the village.

If paved pathways in some areas barely wider than a sidewalk cannot accommodate one of our taxis, then the only other choice is walking. To transport heavier loads such as furniture or for construction purposes, freight vehicles are permitted, some built especially for our local conditions, and helicopters are also commonly used.

Unlike ninety-five percent of guests who arrive in Zermatt by train, these two American guests both drove cars from the nearby town of Täsch to Zermatt on a road marked with a large, red and white *No Entry* sign that had obviously not registered its message. Both had made it to a parking garage at the edge of town meant for car storage for the locals, or for those who had acquired a day permit from the police to drive to the edge of town in exchange for fifty Swiss francs. Both had been lucky to avoid a one hundred Swiss franc fine for traffic violation (increasing to three hundred fifty francs if a car actually enters the village) and an invitation to head back to Täsch.

***

As specific nationalities and cultural groups—Korean, Chinese, Indian, American, etc.—have trooped into my place, one after the other, I could not help but form impressions and associate my observations with various countries of origin and cultures. Even though each guest is a blank slate until he/she arrives, I developed, frankly speaking, prejudices based on origins.

Throughout this book I have put forth personal observations, such as above, and drawn conclusions that I have shared with the reader. This might be termed being "opinionated." The question arises for me, as I am sure it does for the reader, about just how representative or valid these pointed observations and opinions are.

Long before becoming an Airbnb host, I had an interest in how and why people generalize about anything and anybody. On the one hand, it is virtually impossible not to hear generalizations from almost everyone everyday. On the other hand, conscientious individuals are also quick to denounce stereotyping, which is nothing but a generalization. So what's going on?

Routinely encountering tourists in town as well as foreign guests in my home, I now had good reason to examine exactly how or why I arrived at my personal feelings about various guests without much actual, advance knowledge. For example, sad to say, some of my prejudices extend specifically to my Swiss guests, my countrymen. I have come to see them as missing the attributes that I like most in guests, and that I often encounter in other nationalities: easy conversation, openness, shared laughter and flexibility. I link these characteristics now with most of my guests, except for the German-Swiss and also somewhat northward.

I have simply never hosted a taciturn Italian who preferred not to talk, for example. I did have a Swiss woman watch as I went to the bathroom and blew my nose into tissue from a role of toilet paper. The guest noticed and, in all seriousness, proclaimed, "I never thought of using toilet paper to blow my nose. I think there are special tissues for that purpose."

Hark! Indeed there are special tissues just for that purpose. And, in my experience, only the Swiss would remind me of that fact. "You're breaking the rule!"

A do-it-yourself, try something different, and think-out-of-the-box mentality is alien to a culture too used to permanence, stability and well-traveled streets that have remained the same for centuries. And speaking of streets brings me to an observation: there is a noticeable dearth of street signage in smaller Swiss towns. Why would you need street signs? The locals know where everything is.

The fact that I was amassing conclusions and prejudices about guests in advance and based on their origins bothered me to the point where I had to consciously remind myself that the feelings that arise before meeting a guest can be entirely misleading, and they usually were.

Not every American was into drugs; not every Asian person would want to cook noodles; not every Swiss male was unsociable and taciturn during their stay. Also, I fully realized that the issues of stereotyping, prejudice, and generalizations were at the heart of the ease with which fake news and false stories prevail. Of course, this was exactly what I was battling and what I wanted to understand.

I began to wonder what the biological source of prejudice and generalization could be in terms of brain functioning. In my searching I discovered something remarkable and unexpected. Generalizing and prejudice are critically important to intelligent behavior and beneficial to survival. Generalizing reflects normal, healthy brain functioning—leading to feelings that are difficult to eliminate. Those feelings, however, can be brought under rational control by the brain's prefrontal cortex, or intelligence if you will.

How the brain stores memory exemplifies the importance of reaching generalizations, which unavoidably lead to a desire to stereotype.

When remembering any event, shortcuts need to be taken by the brain, as it is impossible and actually counterproductive to remember every detail of a past event. An example that illustrates the point is the memory of being bitten by a dog. Such an incident can occur at a specific time with a specific breed of dog while walking in a specific part of any town. In this case, however, the breed, location and time are not important and the experience is thus simplified (generalized) in actual memory.

The brain has found it advantageous to remember that any dog can bite ... anywhere, anytime. To do this the brain creates what are called engrams. Engrams are traces of memory that are adequate to favor survival in association with reflex reactions in response to new events that resemble a past event in a critical detail: dogs bite and a dog bite hurts.

In the case described above involving Mr. Bill Cosby (actually Dr. Bill Cosby, he has a PhD) and the police, I came to generalize my experience through the painful discovery that a North American woman caused my problem while Asians hadn't. Even though she may have been the only woman, among maybe 200 million possible North American women, who would have called the police for discussing Bill Cosby, my brain was sensitized, and arguably irrationally so.

The formation of an engram involves strengthening connections, called synapses, between select populations of brain cells that are active (firing) during an event. This leads to an expression in neuroscience: synapses that fire together wire together. The wiring-together forms a pattern in memory, and future events do not need to match this pattern exactly to have the pattern, and the feelings, be remembered and acted upon in the future.

The human brain has evolved to store experiences and encounters as memories of incomplete patterns based on outstanding, identifiable characteristics. These patterns are then used for the important process of making predictions—the assumed likely results to be had in the future based on partial, past patterns imbedded from all of the senses.

Anyone can readily see that employing a past pattern, or memory, to predict the future may be entirely irrational. No doubt, following "instincts" in making a decision may feel right, may make us feel in control, but they can also lead to injustice. Yet such decisions seem to often prevail over facts.

The rustling in the bush and a movement in the grass beside you may be a venomous snake only once in one hundred times, but it only takes one in one hundred times to end a life.

Is there statistical justification to predict that rustling in the grass is a snake? Probably not. But the fact that it *could* be a snake makes a deep impression that far outweighs the statistical unlikelihood. Thus, we have the start of an irrational yet advantageous thought, a generalization. The feeling of threat overwhelms any rational conclusion. The usefulness of generalizations is therefore deeply embedded through human evolution and makes them not only useful but also a type of reflex.

The reflex, of course, can be the problem.

Generalizations do lead to a great deal of injustice in the form of prejudice towards an individual who deserves a rational, independent appraisal but gets instead the feelings associated with a pattern, the "rustling in the bush." The art in this has already been well explained and summarized in parts of the brilliant and practical best-selling book by Daniel Kahneman, *Thinking Fast and Slow*: If you're in a race and you pass the runner in second place, what place are you then in? Thinking fast: first place; thinking slow: second place. By far, we are all guilty of thinking too fast.

A prime example of the power of—and the damage done by—generalizations gone amok can readily be extracted from a favorite source, the American legal system. Today, approximately ninety-five percent of all criminal cases are plea-bargained, fundamentally an admission of "non-innocence" by the accused person in lieu of a trial. These cases are thus never adjudicated in court. The ninety-five percent figure is not an indicator of guilt, but instead reflects the ability of the criminal justice system to apply the pressure required for a defendant to concede to a mere accusation.

Every criminal defense lawyer is aware of this important statistic on plea-bargaining; it literally determines the practice of criminal law. To the human lawyer mind, the ninety-five percent figure is as good as saying, "It's going to happen." That is, even if innocent, a defendant will capitulate and the lawyer will not be going to a trial to prove innocence.

Criminal defense lawyers are overwhelmingly influenced by the ninety-five percent statistic and to a potentially catastrophic extent. Why go through the difficult, painstaking task of preparing evidence and witnesses for a trial that isn't going to happen? However, this generalization lands innocent people in prison, and it has done so numerous times, as lawyers failed to prepare adequately. Lawyers relied instead on the pressure that can be applied in last-minute consultations and via their warnings and threats to their own clients. If the pressure fails to result in a plea-bargain, and a stubborn defendant insists on a trial anyway, catastrophe awaits.

A lawyer can trap himself by relying on the highly seductive generalization stemming from what ninety-five percent of defendants feel compelled to do. The lawyer cannot then explain to the judge, "Oh, I need more time now, to prepare, as I had assumed we could pressure this client into a plea-bargain."

In the above sense, a good portion of what we call evil deeds can be attributed simply to how the human mind inadequately handles the nuances of statistical information coming its way. If enough of a pattern exists along with fast thinking, then anyone's individuality can be cast aside in rash judgment.

The five percent of defendants who insist on a trial to prove innocence and refuse to plea bargain are out of luck with too many lawyers; their only crime may have been resisting the ninety-five percent category. The official crime when they are found guilty, however, will be stated otherwise. Past capitulations by clients and the story learned therefrom becomes the effective guide to the future too often.

This example from the legal system, of course, is at the far end of the damage spectrum, but the nature of the mistake that is made, of discounting the unlikely event or the so-called "black swan event" is universal. Absolute conclusions are made based on what is appraised as likely, while discounting that the unlikely is even possible. (For more information on this, see my book *Lawyers Broken Bad* (www.lawyersbrokenbad.com).

I studied the importance of pattern recognition that leads to generalizations in the human brain and the consequent behavior in some depth. It turns out that one of the greatest mysteries in the science of the brain today, and that also happens to be critical to the development of truly intelligent artificial intelligence (and not simply amassing associable data), is how the brain functions so effectively by using a feature called *invariance*. Invariance, by its nature, necessarily results in generalizations.

Generalizations are efficient and advantageous to individual survival. Taking the time to consider all available options when confronting a situation that has stimulated the retrieval of a past pattern is inefficient, costing energy and time. Actions based on the most salient elements can enhance survival.

Gorillas, our closest cousins, have brains far smaller than the human brain. They must spend their entire day eating raw food, while fire and cooked food opened a floodgate of additional nutrients that allowed the human brain to enlarge.

Our brain consumes about twenty-five percent of our total energy usage. Generalizations carried out by the brain save energy by discounting options other than those that aid survival.

Generalization can be said to have led to our survival as intelligent creatures, while at the same time we also scorn it for being the opposite. This explains why, on the one hand and quite naturally, we all fall into making generalizations and, on the other hand, we readily admit intellectually that they may not be justified.

Recently, it has been suggested that the reason why we *Homo sapiens* have prevailed throughout our evolution, while other lines such as *Homo sapiens denisova* or the Neanderthals perished, may well have been our greater ability to act as generalists and thereby to be more adaptable.

Energy savings, survival advantages, and what has emerged as intelligent behavior are entangled with each other; that entanglement favors prejudice, what we see as tribal behavior and stereotyping. These deep attributes of human behavior will not be readily replaced by concepts such as justice for the individual or the minority group. It seems that the good derived from forming generalizations cannot be had without inviting the bad.

What brain characteristic does it take, what special feature is required to be more adaptable, to be a survivor as a generalist?

In simple form, it is the *invariance* mentioned above that leads to generalizations, and this can be conceptualized as follows: (I thank Jeff Hawkins and his fantastic book *On Intelligence* for his insight and my inspiration on this subject.)

Imagine three buckets that we label Red, Green and Blue. You are given the job of placing colored pieces of paper that come your way into one of these three buckets. Usually this is not a problem because, for the simplistic example presented here, we will assume that most colors encountered are red, green or blue, or close, easily identifiable shades of these.

Now, along comes the color yellow. Well, there is no Yellow bucket. To make a special bucket called Yellow takes time and effort better seen as spent on other activities, given how infrequently yellow comes along. So yellow gets placed in, for example, the Green bucket (a form of "thinking fast"). The contents of the Green bucket then get passed up the decision-making line to higher centers of the brain, where weightier decisions are made based on differing criteria. There, critical decisions about yellow are made based on the nature of the bucket that it came from, i.e. it came from the Green bucket. Now, causation can be attributed, but incorrectly: that piece of paper was in the Green bucket because it was green.

In terms of the example given above from the legal system, yellow represents the five percent of defendants who wish to go to trial to claim innocence and refuse the plea bargain; guilt or innocence becomes irrelevant and is dismissed because yellow landed in the Green bucket. Those individuals are treated as green.

Here is the big problem for the human brain: it would be impossible for it not to compartmentalize information that leads to generalizations and still remain efficient at ensuring survival in a given environment. We are therefore wired to generalize, all of us, even the best among us.

Consider the following statements: The Chinese are an "industrious, filthy, obtuse people" who "don't sit on benches while eating, but squat like Europeans do when they relieve themselves out in the leafy woods." They are "a peculiar herd-like nation, often more like automatons than people." And finally, "It would be a pity if these Chinese supplant all other races, for the likes of us the mere thought is unspeakably dreary."

Who might have made such wild, sweeping, negative statements devoid of adequate forethought about a vast ethnic group? A white supremacist? A neo-Nazi or KKK member? Some other *Dumbkopf*? No, none other than the renowned humanitarian, philosopher and deep-thinking genius, Albert Einstein. The above quotes were all taken directly from his diary.

In contrast to Einstein's off-the-cuff remarks, a more recent example of far-reaching, systematic generalization comes from Harvard University. In its application process, Harvard consistently rated Asian-Americans inferior to other Harvard applicants in categories such as "courage," and "positive personality," "likability," "kindness," and being "widely respected." These determinations were made across more than 160,000 student records. The 160,000 figure here might at first glance mislead and seem to lend support as some sort of statistical justification for the generalizations that were made. But note, are there objective tests for courage, kindness and likability in the first place?

It seems likely that courage, for example, can only truly be measured in the act. There may be quite a few people who declare that they will rush into a burning building to save a trapped child. How many will do so on the occasion? Or how many lawyers will tell a defendant they will go all the way to a trial on their behalf in legal defense when the client first walks in the office, only to shrink from such when the disclosure of evidence requires confronting peers or possible career damage, or the effort of going to trial is just too burdensome?

I doubt that Harvard set up burning buildings or any other real-life situation to determine a response that would allow for a conclusion about the level of any groups' courage, Asian or otherwise. As was once famously said, "God gave man language so that he could conceal his thoughts."

I am reminded of a survey taken of Korean students who scored at the highest level in the world on math tests. When they were asked whether they were good at math, humility prevailed. The students put forth that they were not very good. At the same time, American students—who ranked far lower on the same tests—answered that they were very good at math.

So what can an interview really tell us about such qualities as courage or kindness if an equivalent basis of understanding is lacking at a verbal level? Obviously, people both smart and dumb, good and bad are in the habit of making generalizations. They do this often as a mental reflex. After all, how can an "I really don't know" answer to any question suffice and lead to respect for that person?

But we need to be careful on this point:

In the 1980's two neuroscientists, Michael Gazzaniga and Roger Sperry, performed an experiment that, from its interpretation forward, would forever undermine our ability to claim objectivity in verbally describing reality. They showed two pictures to a patient who had the connection between the two hemispheres of his brain cut in order to control epileptic seizures. That is, the two halves of the brain no longer had any way of communicating with each other. By partitioning the view for each eye of the patient, the left hemisphere saw only a picture of a chicken foot, the right hemisphere was shown a wintry, snowy scene. The patient was next shown a series of photos (toothbrush, shovel, chicken, fork) visible to both eyes (both hemispheres). He was then asked to associate the photos with the chicken foot and the snowy scene. For the chicken foot, the patient chose the photo of a chicken, and for the snowy scene the shovel. All was as it should be.

The scientists then asked the patient *why* he picked the chicken and the shovel images. He explained: the chicken foot belongs to the chicken, and the shovel... is used to clean out the chicken shed!

The right hemisphere was exposed to the photo of the snowy scene, but it has no verbal abilities and could not communicate with the verbal, left hemisphere. The snowy scene registered unconsciously. The patient, however, did not respond by saying "I don't know" when asked why he picked the shovel. Instead, the left hemisphere, which the scientists called the "interpreter," made up a verbal story that related to reality ... not in the slightest! This was pure, pedestrian rationalization.

This experiment has been repeated many times with the same result. The left brain, the verbal hemisphere, invents stories to make sense of incoming information after the fact. It appears that the human brain has evolved to prioritize a world that makes internal sense in the context of our own memories and experiences. And that story can be influenced by many factors, not least of all by fear.

We expect of ourselves and others that there should always be some reference point to make a pronouncement on reality based on memory and experience, and we often extrapolate and merely act on that reference point alone. We often call a person who does so "confident" or even a "bold leader." This was certainly a common reaction to, for example, President George W. Bush when he proclaimed that he made decisions based on "my gut." The same is true of President Trump.

Take religion as an example. How many people are willing to say, "I don't know" to the question of the existence of God or what the true religion is? It is extraordinary to consider that circumstances of chance alone, i.e. being born into a certain culture or religion, have led so many children of Muslims, Hindus, Christians and Jews to also become Muslims, Hindus, Christians and Jews and solely thereby to answer religious questions the same as their parents, and to conclude that those answers are the correct answers!

Not only is it more satisfying to rely on "gut instinct" than to say, "I don't know," it is also viewed as a strength and a quality of leadership. We might come to accept grudgingly that the wisest of men will say, "I don't know" on some subject. Some such men are called, for example, Buddhist monks. Note that they do not typically serve in positions of leadership or power.

Generalizing and telling ourselves the story that makes the most sense is wholly natural to the human mind, a reflex borne not of the intellect but of the lower brain regions readily gaining salience through natural upper brain laziness, or plain thoughtlessness because having just the right "bucket" available takes time, effort and energy. The brain prefers to fill-in partial patterns automatically when encountering the outlines of a story.

It isn't often considered this way, but failing to reach a conclusion in the face of existing patterns that have entered the brain through the senses in the past, and that may say absolutely nothing worthwhile about circumstance in the present or future, requires more cognitive effort than reaching the intuitive conclusion that may be miles wrong. That is, fighting against an ingrained pattern requires more effort by the brain.

An example of the difficulty of unlearning an established pattern comes from the study of bilingual language abilities. Research in this area shows that the brain must exert greater cognitive effort in stopping the use of the vocabulary of one language—that is, ignoring that specific neuronal pattern—than in starting the use of another language. As the preacher once said, "I could make my sermons shorter, but once I get started I find that I'm too lazy to stop."

So Einstein, like everyone else, fell into the trap of (or the predilection for) easy, fast thinking. But note:

while generalizations are not borne of the intellect, they can be controlled by the more advanced part of the brain, the prefrontal cortex. That is why we have a big brain, to use it. Using it is the job of a modern, educated human.

Think as you like, feel as you are inclined, but act as you should for a just world. And anyway, wouldn't old Al Einstein be surprised today by a trip to Shanghai? Somewhere along the way, when maybe no one was looking, the "Chinese fire drills" of lore became a whole lot more organized.

***

The natural inclination of the brain to generalize results in some highly consequential impacts. Outstanding practical examples of this again occur routinely in our legal system. For example, true or not, the prosecution at a trial can put forth an implied framework of a defendant's drug use, irresponsibility and unemployment, to be hung around the neck of a black defendant sitting before a jury. Is it likely that the black defendant is a physicist? Even if he is, that would not match the pattern, the story that we have been taught to recognize. Whether or not the defendant committed the crime as charged, we recognize the pattern and the implied story suggested to us by the prosecution. That pattern seduces us far more than slogging through the facts and allowing those facts to change our thinking.

Today, in many regards—climate issues, politics, vaccinations—we are faced with the conundrum of people unwilling to make judgments based on facts but rather on stories that suit them. A reference back to the fundamentals of the brain is the only way to make sense of this.

To change a mind, or to alter an entrenched belief or

depart from an established pattern, some form of "pain" may need to be navigated. Asking someone why they cannot accept facts can be equivalent to asking, "Why are you hesitating to put your hand on that hot stove?"

It was Swiss psychiatrist Elizabeth Kübler-Ross who pointed out, albeit indirectly, that adapting to a new way of thinking—in her specific experience the acceptance of death by her near-death patients—required transiting five emotional stages: denial, anger, bargaining, depression, acceptance. Those are also stages in change of mind; they can be formidable because of the emotional pain involved.

Allowing facts to change an established pattern is a rocky path upward to find some elusive truth. Pattern completion through generalization is the easy, downhill path to comfortable believability.

It would be a major advance if we consciously recognized that facts may be—and may actually need to be—subordinate to false beliefs for a time (because a listener to those facts may not tolerate the pain), or at least that can be the case upon first encountering a fact-based story that does not please us.

The idea of pattern recognition and the desire for completion of the pattern from personal memory can also be readily understood in the context of music. Recently, I listened to a brass band on a headset prior to falling sleep. At the start of the music I could not discern any pattern at all. My memory could not square the sounds that I heard with a piece of music that I was familiar with. But suddenly, the pattern emerged as the recognizable *When the Saints Go Marching In*. The name and the known melody allowed me to immediately stop the work of scanning for something recognizable. I predicted the future at that point, the expected melody to come. I knew the flow and how it would end. But, alas, I was wrong in my prediction. And why did I even make such a prediction in the first place? After all, a band can do as it wishes. Indeed, the band then switched over and went on to several other melodies. It's a similar situation with the "sounds" of stories. We often complete them with less than all the facts.

Recent neuroscience research identifies two ways in which humans anticipate or predict the future: one type of anticipation relies on our memories from past experiences, the other on rhythm, as with knowing the rhythm of music in advance. Two different brain anatomical sites are involved: the cerebrum for memory, the cerebellum and a deeper brain structure known as the basal ganglia for rhythm.

Herein also resides the tale of the allure and power of fake news: handing us an easy, well-known melody. Fake news exploits the path of least brain resistance and leads a listener down along it.

This knowledge only reinforces why I avoid telling my personal story to strangers. The "armed and dangerous, internationally wanted criminal" category is too seductive; it fills into a bucket far easier to load than creating a special bucket that complicates a simple, easier understanding of how the world works.

Awareness of this phenomenon through exploration of the scientific literature also led me to question the generalizations that I was forming with regard to my Airbnb guests, their origins, cultures and habits.

I continually ponder whether the patterns that I see exhibited by guests are meaningful in terms of actual generalizations that hold overall merit. I am thankful to be able to engage in that process knowingly. It does, however, require greater effort.

XIV.   Mao, Mao, Mao

"Not friends, not enemies, just strangers with some memories."
~ Daniel Blum, Irish DJ, producer, and singer

How many women are eager to go on a date with an international fugitive? How many can comprehend the strange story that I might tell without healthy skepticism? Even so, there are two slinky felines in Zermatt who care not a lick about my internet profile.

Each day I walk up the steep hill to my home in the shadow of our great mountain, lugging an armful of groceries. I am often met by two distinctly different female characters, one tabby and one ginger.

Ginger, as I call her, casts me a sideways glance whenever she sees me. Sizing me up, she pretends to walk away, but she is really waiting for what she knows is coming and indeed anticipates: a neck rub along her collar, a long stroke of her fine, orange-tinted fur, and the gentle grasp of her tail. Quickly content with that amount of attention, she scampers away maybe a few meters, then hangs around waiting, looking back; we do it all over again.

To Ginger the world appears good. Maybe more importantly the world has been good to her; she is full of trust. We part each other's company with all being in order until we meet again. Not so, however, with Tabby.

I run into Tabby about as often as I do Ginger, but we never touch. She senses my intent as soon as she sees me, freezes, and then off she scampers, looking back as if to say it wasn't meant to be for you and me. Anyway, when are *you* going to pull my tail too hard or send a stone in my direction? That stopping and looking back … I wonder why she does that? To make sure that I keep my distance or some other reason?

I think more about Tabby than I do about Ginger. That is in the way of human nature. The memories of what Ginger and I have will never amount to the memories of what Tabby and I will never have.

I know Ginger's history. All happy cats, as someone once said, are happy in the same way. But all cats like Tabby have been treated badly differently. Maybe kicked by a thirteen-year-old boy, or suffered through a frightening charge with stamping feet that came her way. Or maybe she was stepped on as a kitten, with no, "Oh, I am so sorry little kitty. Here, let's give you some warm milk."

I have often wondered if Tabby is destined to never enjoy what Ginger enjoys so readily. Did the thirteen-year-old boy have such power, to put Tabby on an unalterable course… for life? If only I could have her understand, "Look, Tabby, not everyone does those things …" But you can't talk to a cat. In fact, you can't really just talk to most people, either.

It isn't good enough to tell an abused child, "I will not hurt you." The point of inflection and infliction may be lost to change forever. What Tabby and others like her needed was a hero, a hero who never appeared, who could have stopped the shock and pain before it altered them so.

Be assured, Ginger and I are good friends and we will stay that way. But Tabby, well, she brings sadness out in me, and an odd longing. I wish I could teach her what she can't learn.

Then, I happened to meet Lingce. The meeting didn't result through Airbnb, but female Airbnb Asian guests had sensitized me to the allure of Asian women.

Before hosting through Airbnb I had favorable impressions of a few Asians with whom I had worked in the distant past, but I had no social or personal experiences to go by. As more than fifty percent of my guests were Asian, I began to view them with considerable respect, admiration and affection. Those who visited me were polite, often endearingly affectionate guests with well-developed senses of humor, but could also be serious minded. They did not act jaded, as some of my American guests did even under the Matterhorn. They allowed themselves to appear in wonderment. They often brought small gifts of appreciations from their countries. Far, indeed, from the stereotype of the stern, inhuman Asian left over from the days when communism was our greatest threat.

I recall two Japanese women who once embarrassed me by offering to help me clean the apartment. This was not meant in any way as a slight, or as a hint. It was their way of showing kindness and respect. Of course, I turned down the offer. Nevertheless, they kept right on bowing. The level of concern for their host, while they were paying me, made a deep impression.

The likelihood of such an offer being made by an American? I suggest zero.

An interesting observation comes to mind. Chinese and American study participants were asked to observe a video that was specially set up to show an aquarium scene with a lone fish swimming apart from a group of fish. Americans characterized the lone fish as likely being dominant and powerful, while Chinese interpreted the same scene with sympathy for the lone fish; they viewed it as having been excluded from the group. I can see a bit of this as Asian guests arrive—cooperating, getting along and pleasing me as a host seem to be priorities. We are all quickly "the home team."

Because many Asians visiting me are traveling for the first time, they are buoyed in spirit by the newness and wonder of seeing things up close that they had heard so much about and perhaps never expected to be able to visit. That leads to contagious, positive radiation.

I felt attracted to the delicacy, femininity and kindness shown to me by Asian women. They appear to be less self-conscious about putting forward an image that is traditional and perhaps traditionally favored by men, and appear less concerned with competing with a man. This contrasted with the gender power politics that exist today between so many American men and women, and that I had become negatively sensitized to.

I have spent considerable time thinking about why I should be so taken by Asian women. Was I merely a superficial Western man impressed by what might frankly be called obvious subservience? Did femininity have to mean that a woman had to play the submissive role? Was what I viewed as femininity just short-lived catnip of a sort that would come to hallmark an extended relationship with a woman who would accept less equality and sharing, and would tolerate my greater independence?

This exact topic, of the attraction of Asian women, made the opinion column of the *New York Times* recently, courtesy of controversial remarks by the French novelist and filmmaker, Yann Moix. Mr. Moix, in addition to stating in an interview in the French magazine *Marie Clair* that he did not wish to sleep with women over age fifty, also claimed that he preferred Asian women. French critics accused him of "probably buying into the pernicious stereotype that they're submissive."

The problem with such issues is that they pit the rational against what we can call the biological. In a contest between the two, the biological always wins initially, then perhaps is chased away by the rational when it is too late. Such issues are on an intellectual plane. Too intellectual to influence an initial decision-making process.

The fact is, emotions rule male-female relationships. If you like someone, you like them and that is it. Does anyone think that Mr. Moix will change his carnal desires based on argumentation? Whatever the basis for the attraction, what I saw I generally liked in the Asian women who visited me.

As mentioned above, I came to judge the favorability of my guests not only by the level of the conversations that arose, but also by the emotions or passions that they expressed for whatever the subject might be. On this basis, I never expected much from my northern European guests beyond the intellectual. The South Americans, Italians, Greeks and the Spanish, that was another story. These folks love to talk and tell me how they feel about everything. But I will never forget two young Chinese ladies, studying journalism and mass communications at a university in England, who came to visit me after traveling from St. Moritz on the famous Glacier Express train.

Now, anyone over a certain age remembers the image of young Chinese women from Mao-era CBS news clips: unemotional, no-nonsense types dressed in military garb, Mao caps, and ready to invade *your* village with communist fervor. Every time I meet a modern day Chinese woman, I recall those news clips and have to smile. *It ain't like that no more.* Today, *bai shou mei* (white, thin, beautiful), as inspired by the capitalist West, has replaced the feminine ideal of sturdy and strong of Mao's time.

Vivacious and bubbly, chicly dressed and sharp as razors, I knew from the start that Olivia and Shiya, both from mainland China, would keep me interested not only with their keen observations, but also with their curiosity and questions. They had no problems connecting immediately on a personal level.

The evening of their arrival, after dinner, I asked them whether they would like to watch a movie, and what kind of movies did they like? Both answered in favor of … romantic. So we settled on watching *Love Actually,* which they had never seen. At first, it appeared that they lacked interest in the movie, checking their phones for messages more than watching. But as relationships on screen began to develop with more emotion, their interest picked up and became apparent and focused.

By the end of the film, to my amazement and amusement, both sat on my sofa, tears streaming down their cheeks and the most intense looks of concentration on their faces. I brought them a roll of toilet paper. (I never do this with a Swiss guest!) Olivia grabbed it from my hand in utter desperation, without acknowledging that I handed it to her, and the blowing began.

The two of them were completely hooked by the developing story, in love with the characters and as vulnerable as straw huts in a Beijing windstorm. I couldn't help but think, *Does General Secretary Xi Jinping really think he will make it as dictator for life in China?* The China that walks into my living room says, "hardly."

***

When I met Lingce, I had well-developed notions of what a relationship with an Asian woman would be like. She was Chinese, Hong Kong Chinese to be exact. I met her while she and I were traveling on the train from Zermatt to Interlaken. I wasn't surprised when I saw she had a picture of a fluffy, white pet rabbit with a bow around its neck, rather than her own photo on her Skype profile. It fit her shyness and porcelain China-doll fragility. My attraction for her was instant; I pursued her via email after she returned home, one day after meeting her.

When Lingce finally responded to my emails after a period of total silence, daily chats began regularly via Skype. Ten o'clock Zermatt time corresponded with the time when her boss, at a freight-forwarding company in Hong Kong, left the office. The mice will play, as they say.

Lingce's voice matched her porcelain features ... soft, vulnerable, with a pale quality. It could be slow and measured because of a reticence borne of what I thought was her question to the world: Do I have a right to draw attention? It had not taken me long to recognize that this was indeed being asked. I was just the opposite. I was attracted to the shy and the reluctant; I felt good as their champion. So it was obvious to me, the two of us made a pair.

The rabbits Lingce raised back home also made sense, the fact that she had them as pets. They harmed no one, but were readily slaughtered. As it turned out, she had been their champion.

At thirty-eight years of age there were no children in Lingce's life. But then, from nowhere, something emerged that appeared out of character and disturbing: She expressed open hostility toward children.

"The world has enough children," she proclaimed angrily when the topic arose. That disdain troubled me. I like children. And at another time she said, "I hope there are no children there," referring to an upcoming social event to which she had been invited in Hong Kong. (Her comments reminded me of a troubled female guest who stunned me one day by saying that she had deliberately knocked down a child on a ski piste. "I didn't try to avoid her, she was in my way; I knocked her right over," she had declared forthrightly.)

Combined with Lingce's fragility, there were also sporadic hints of deep anger. But when her remarks illustrated harshness too evident, twenty-four hours later an email would arrive in my mailbox, with an explanation, regret, and then a retraction—a plea for reconsideration.

Lingce sensed that kindness was expected of her, and surely she wanted to offer it, to have it prevail. Otherwise, it was too much like staking her claim on the world. More delightful, though, was a stirring sassiness that she possessed that could just as readily emerge. Sort of a flip side, by which she exhibited Chinese-style toughness. When I teased her about Mao Tse Tung, she bridled.

"Don't mention him again or I will stop talking to you; he was a terrible man," she threatened.

When, a bit later, I sent her an email with an oblique reference to Mao, meant to tease, she warned me again. I defended myself facetiously, claiming, "Mao ... that's just the sound that a cat makes: mao, mao, mao."

Lingce shot back at the speed of light. "Very clever ... you a liar!"

The repartee was playful and spirited and I enjoyed it immensely. Here were two people, two entirely different cultures, trying out their memories, their personal histories on one another, seeking that level playing field, the right fit.

For three months on most weekdays I faithfully and eagerly talked with Lingce for at least an hour a day, and often more. There was plenty to talk about. I helped her improve her English, reading to her from a book. Lingce dutifully kept a list of new words that she was learning from the readings. I was impressed.

One day, Lingce asked about a book she had heard about. The title was something like *Love Yourself More*. She was curious; she asked me what I thought the title meant. I volunteered that, apparently, some people needed to like themselves more, so that they could feel lovable, and maybe love someone else.

"It must be a self-help book," I guessed, and thought no more about it. Miss the point of the question entirely I did. Lingce's curiosity had a reason. It should have turned into a better conversation.

How often does one person throw a lifeline to another in the hope that it will be grasped, only to have it drop and be abandoned in murky waters? It had happened more than once in my life, that I had missed an important signal from another person. That was how relationships stalled and then drifted away. Of course, I hadn't known it then.

One day Lingce asked me, "Does knowing intellectually about patterns of behavior in relationships help someone have a good relationship?"

I reflected on this, then replied, "No, not really."

Lingce let out a murmur of affirmation. Obviously, there had been failures in her life.

"It's two different parts of the brain you're dealing with," I proposed. "It's being in one room, forced to guess what's happening in a completely different room. Maybe it helps to understand, or to rationalize post facto, after a relationship has ended. But by then you have a different environment. The environment of a relationship, the emotional closeness, is not an environment that comes under rational control."

Talk to someone almost every day for an hour or so; talk to them about things in life that really matter, things like favorite music, beautiful places in this world to visit, various animal and pet issues, difficulties at work. After three months you begin to think you know a person, and a desire arises for closeness from both sides.

Lingce accepted my invitation to visit Zermatt. She was able to swing one week of leave, booked her flight, and the sublime joy of expectation and planning began.

For three months, minds had had a good meeting. I looked forward to face-to-face talk, the natural progression of what had been building. *But is the anticipation mutual,* I wondered?

Of course, there was that ever-lingering threat of disappointment, of change of mind. There was always the possibility that Lingce was a long-distance tease. More than likely, in fact. She had warned me ... no, she had scorned me when I suggested she was the adventurous type, for her love of traveling and now this risk-taking.

"Hah," she contradicted, "I am certainly not courageous."

Then why plan to visit a man you met for just several hours on a train? That takes some degree of courage.

It is said that folks from Hong Kong are enthusiastic, proficient shoppers. This proved so true of Lingce. She put the greatest effort—I could hear the thrill of it in her voice—shopping creatively for gifts to bring based on some of my inquiries about Hong Kong foods and various fabrics.

Lingce reveled in telling me what she intended to

bring to Zermatt from Hong Kong. The gifts and the shopping, these efforts showed touching concern for making her Skype partner happy. It moved me considerably, this caring on open display. This woman had feelings and acted on them. In turn, hearing of all of the intended gifts, I made it understood that payment would be due for such treasure. I suspected Lingce did not earn much money, working as an accountant at a small company.

I was highly receptive to the enthusiasm on Lingce's part, her desire to make a good impression on her arrival. Despite H. L. Mencken's warning that love is the delusion that one woman differs from another, I began to imagine that this woman, deep down, was special. I also imagined other things. I had, of course, already seen her body clothed, that Chinese slim, with long black hair and delicate facial features, precisely defined, sharper than was typical.

Unrealistic expectations, it was mutually agreed in our conversations, were the cause of too many problems between people.

"No expectations, when I come," Lingce demanded, more like a promise to herself maybe. "Just have fun, a good time," she reaffirmed. I remained silent. I had expectations, but "just for fun" would do for starters.

The trip to Zermatt was planned for late February. One day, Lingce excitedly called me to say she just might come early, right at Christmas, in over a week's time. I had initially suggested a Christmas visit, Christmas in Zermatt, but I had given up on the idea. Wasn't practical. Now, suddenly, it seemed possible. It was a bit of *carpe diem* on Lingce's part. But I had to explain that, while the idea was welcome, I had since accepted a writing project for a client that would take up that time. It would be a shame not to devote all of my attention to her. Twenty-four hours later, Lingce admitted her urge was too impulsive.

"Yes, it's better if I don't come for Christmas."

But the planned February visit turned into an earlier January visit, while she was able to somehow keep February on the books as well, she explained.

Clearly, there was enough interest by now on her part to convince me that close companionship might emerge from a chance meeting on a train.

The big day in January arrived. It was cold, gray and blustery at the train station where we met, a ten-minute walk from the apartment. After months of talking, there was this new, physical presence. Where there had been two voices at a distance, now there was proximity, walking together, seeing the other person's reactions, physical closeness and the issue of just how close.

What appraisals are made, when two people of the opposite sex meet? Always and ever derived from memories. Some call it baggage—that human feature wrongly thought of as merely the key to the past, when memories are the compass to the future.

Could memory be considered a sense? Like vision or hearing? I thought about that. Sight provides information, hearing provides information, and so do memories. They can limit us, or protect us. "Oh, I ordered salmon once in a restaurant, and I got sick. I'm not going to order that any more." It makes no sense at all, but sense isn't what counts.

The two of us hugged briefly at the train station, then walked the ten minutes up the mountain to my place.

When I first touched Lingce in the apartment, gently on the shoulders, she recoiled.

"Calm down, calm down," she instructed.

There was already calm, the touching was meant only as admiration, not as something to continue at that moment. The porcelain Chinese woman had decided to visit a stranger, and had never wavered, never prevaricated, never teased. That had taken courage. It demanded admiration.

And then there was the boatload of gifts: Chinese slippers, socks, a wallet, Gator snow leggings, BBQ beef jerky (the finest I have ever tasted), tea from Sri Lanka with a heavenly, light flavor, a shopping bag full of spices and noodles. Christmas in January. Some of the items had been requested. Most not. What was obvious was the time these purchases had taken, the thoughtfulness.

Yet something soon arose as drastically wrong. A palpable discontent set in. Unhappiness showed on Lingce's face like coffee stains on a white tablecloth. Was it the light touch on the shoulder? Not by the usual standards. How could it be? Later, a sweet kiss on the cheek, also not welcome. I was confused. I did not persist when rebuffed. Instead, expectations lowered. Perhaps she noticed, maybe not. Probably.

The fear might as well have been fog, the way it settled in on both of us, preventing new incoming information, merely using the old. Suddenly, everything was being compared to back home in Hong Kong. Zermatt, the here and now, came up short in the comparison.

Overt discontent, and then emotional paralysis. Our talking eroded. The food, the restaurants, the local habits—all were inferior here, she found. It was obvious that Lingce had much to say, but say it directly she did not.

On the third day of Lingce's visit I walked into the bathroom to find something that haunts me to this day.

The shiny, flawlessly mirrored steel surface of the toilet paper holder contained hair-thin but distinct scratches doodled across the surface. I froze in place, staring. *Those scratches are new,* I realized. They noticeably marred a formerly perfect surface. I had wiped that surface once every day or more; these scratches were permanent. There were only two people in the apartment. *Could I be wrong?* I looked again, hard. Suddenly, I felt a chill. Something was very wrong.

Oh, this world promises us perfection because we assemble it just so in our minds. Every lover should be perfect because we need and deserve perfection, never mind our own flaws. Now, there was this numbness. It had all turned wrong so quickly.

No, I had to be wrong. Lingce could not have put those scratches there. I left the bathroom and planned the day. Lingce made it obvious, silently, that there was no enthusiasm for any of the planned activities.

It had snowed the day earlier. The two of us hiked a trail to the far end of town, the Matterhorn end. We began an ascent through what were rolling green meadows in summer but under their cover now, and then we headed into a forest of larch trees totally bare of their deciduous needles this time of year.

Someone leaving you psychologically is like helplessly watching them drown in an ocean ten feet away. There is no life preserver, no rope, no effort you can make to bring them back.

Lingce went deep inside her own world as we walked, my efforts at some sort of reunion failing entirely. What I remember today is how the snow sculptures and especially the mini cornices devoured her attention. If I had to guess I would say she had turned ten years old again, as her arms swayed carelessly back and forth, eyes refusing to meet mine. I had, through my efforts at emotional closeness, put her there.

That night, following a meal in one of the higher-priced eating establishments, her frustrations erupted again in the form of displeasure with the menu and the meal; it wasn't being served as it would have been in Hong Kong. Next to me, on the sofa later while watching a movie, Lingce expressed anger openly; she could not understand the English being spoken.

I went to the kitchen to prepare hot chocolate, came back and planted a light kiss on her cheek. It was as if a run-away car had careened into the room right then. A sudden, overwhelming explosion of rage.

"You treat me like a woman of the street," she screamed as she rose to her feet. The absurdity of the statement had me reflexively laugh out loud. My feelings for Lingce were too far removed from her accusation. *She cannot be serious, a tender, friendly kiss on the cheek?*

"And you don't even say you're sorry," she followed up.

"I will certainly not apologize," I countered, "for what, exactly ... for liking you?"

It was as if a juicy steak dinner were being thrown out because a mosquito had landed on the edge of the plate, yet right there she decided to leave. It was surreal, but it was happening.

Lingce went for her belongings and began packing. I remained in place on the sofa. A wave of nausea welled-up. *Leaving? After three days? A disaster after only three days? At the mildest sign of casual affection? It can't be true.*

The packing continued. The suddenness and the apparent groundlessness of the action made it other-worldly.

I objected, "But why... why are you so angry?"

In tears, Lingce physically shuddered, "You don't understand."

Of course I did not understand.

I would not apologize for my display of affection, but at the door, as a last plea, I promised, "Please don't do this. Not like this. I won't touch you again."

Such a retreat by Lingce was inconceivable. After all of the kindness and generosity displayed on her part? It was certainly a retrenchment from her claim of "no expectations" and "just have fun."

Where did such resolve come from? How did a tender kiss of friendship lead to this? It was ten at night.

It was cold outside. Lingce had a large suitcase. The path down to town was steep. Take the suitcase from her? Start a scene in the hallway? There was some poison here. Could it be extracted by confrontation, or would retreat be best to draw it out?

I knew a mother. Her son, Frank, was a drug addict, twenty-five years worth. She continually told everyone that her son would fail to clean up and that he needed her. She protected him all his life, from the failure she knew would follow if he attempted to achieve that which he obviously could not. She knew in her heart that he could not live without her because he was an addict.

"He will surely die ..." if she didn't do this or that for him, she explained.

How could she be so sure? I often wondered. Given that he is now dead due to his addiction, we will never know whether Frank would have had more of a chance at life if his mother had let him try at it on his own.

I would be the last to claim that I made a rational, considered decision about Lingce that night, about whether to act or to remain passive. I was stunned into inaction, like the deer abruptly confronted by a hunter. I watched silently as Lingce, angry and hurt, left the apartment.

Months of hope had been undone in this final stroke of discontentment. Now, it was mental struggle time. What had happened had to make sense, but it did not.

I went into the bathroom, sat on the lid of the toilet, and looked again in confusion at the toilet paper holder. There should have been a confrontation earlier. She had been cruel, but not just to me. She had been crueler to herself.

Two days later Lingce sent an email: "I felt pressure. I know you are angry. I want to thank you for the good food at your home."

I never replied to that email. I needed time. Anger was indeed an option. Some response like, "You have destroyed everything, how could you do that?" was never considered, however. In truth, Lingce was entirely in the wrong, but wrong about assuming that I was angry. Obviously, she expected anger. It was the toilet-paper holder that precluded the anger.

The toilet-paper holder featured a hard, metal-plate surface. Inadvertent scratches were impossible. How? Those scratches were put there by a woman deeply frightened and under emotional pressure in my home, yet I had missed reacting properly to the desperation. I had not confronted her when I first saw the scratches because I had no idea what to make of them. I lacked adequate understanding. My attempts at closeness had only made things worse.

***

After Lingce left, the process of entering the dark reaches of the mind began. It was the dramatic reversal of expectations, the rejection and loss that set my memories off on their wild ride, an independent journey separate of my will. Anger on my part might have forestalled this, but then only made it worse.

Lingce's unhappiness and the dissatisfaction with Zermatt, of course, were also indications of her dissatisfaction with me. There had been great happiness on her part before meeting me for a second time. Almost immediately after our meeting, the sadness had begun. There had not been enough good about me, I felt, to break through some barrier. Instead, the barrier grew higher.

"You only think I am attractive because there are no other women around here," she had once rebuffed me when I told her she looked pretty.

Just as I recognized my own pain and self-doubt from the failed, few days, I would, in the coming days and weeks, recognize that if I had a pained heart, clearly Lingce already had one broken badly.

There were so many fault-deflecting reactions for me to have. "That woman was emotionally disturbed" was the obvious one. I learned long ago that everyone is emotionally disturbed, including me. It was about the same as saying someone was human. In fact, I treasure the eloquent quote attributed to a long-standing president of the American Psychological Association, a man now deceased, on this topic: "Everybody's fucking crazy." You just need the proper environment to bring it out.

Several weeks later, Lingce sent another message. "How are you?" Again, I did not reply. That message was quickly followed by another, "You want nothing more to do with me. Got it."

I did not reply. I still did not know what to say.

I wondered, when someone acts are they acting as

who they are, or are they acting as who they were? And tomorrow, they will act as who they were today, but not as who they are then. They aren't who they are then; they are then who they were. There is no real now; the present is an ever-emergent property arising from the past but only to be seen tomorrow. Everyone is who they were; no one is who they are. Otherwise, endings would not have the power that they have. Process an experience first, become who you are later, rationalize that experience as thought, forever catching up except for once.

The toilet-paper holder remains scratched to this day. I rarely avoid thinking about Lingce when I clean it. The protective coating around her was harder than that stainless steel surface as she reached for some implement to dig away at it. What had she used in my bathroom to grind into it with such fury?

What could have led Lingce to be so terrified of affection and closeness? The question, combined with my memory of the child she was—enjoying the snow sculptures, knocking them down one by one, arms swaying like the child she had become—caused waves of sorrow to pass through me. I wept for Lingce and for my loss of her. Lingce had become my Tabby cat.

Lingce had left some of her clothing behind. These sat in the closet like a smoldering fire, not extinguishable and not ignorable. But wasn't that her own fault, for leaving in an unconsidered rush?

There were two sweaters, both new and obviously purchased to show off. Lingce would surely want them back, but she would be too embarrassed to ask for them.

I put together a package. Several weeks later I contacted her, told her I hoped she was well, and shipped her things back to Hong Kong, along with a gift of some homemade gingerbread.

There was no mellowing on Lingce's part. For some human damage there may be no repair. After Lingce expressed thanks for the return of her goods and I said goodbye, we never spoke again.

Where do people go when they part? What happens in the mind, or to the mind, when someone leaves with no promise of reunion? For me, I regained the image of my mother when I must have been about five years old. She cried at the kitchen table, in her constant homesickness for her father and relatives back in Europe. All these years later I understood her as never before.

Mini-deaths all. Each one reminds of death, the only outcome in any case.

XV.   Eagle's Nest

*"Snow brings a special quality with it—
the power to stop life as you know it dead in its tracks."*
~ Nancy Hatch Woodward, American writer and
journalist

For the first time in many years, Zermatt was dumped on mightily in January 2018 by a massive snowstorm, in this case a relatively rare southeasterly flow of wind known to locals as the *Rofel*. It bore down on us with tons of frozen moisture and barreled into our mountain retreat—with our one-way in and same way out rail and road transportation system. This storm hit us with over one meter of snow, followed by another meter and a half within about one week from a similar storm.

For countless guests all along, I had been providing assurance that no one needed to worry about being snowed-in, here in the valley of the Matterhorn.

"The Swiss with snow are like fish with water," I promised sincerely. "They, of all people, know how to live well with snow." But everything in life comes with a caveat. The winter season of 2018 proved me a big liar.

Formerly visible rooftop chimneys basically disappeared. Walkways narrowed to one lane. Early morning rumblings in the distance were occasionally heard, as intentional acoustic booms loosened accumulated snow from steep mountainsides to prevent avalanches later that might trap skiers. Massive avalanches or the immanent threat of such cut off all land travel. For a total of six days in January, the only way in or out of Zermatt was by helicopter, but they were often prevented from flying due to abundant fog and clouds.

This situation could not be helped, as protecting the entire rail line and single roadway from avalanches was practically impossible. What was shocking, however, was how village administration handled the snowfall locally: they didn't.

Zermatt's main street, our lifeline, was one deep, sloppy morass of slush and underlying ice that should never have been allowed to accumulate in the first place. Meaningful snow removal remained absent for days. People slipped and some were seriously injured. I wondered how long that could go on. This is a tourist village obviously not suffering from lack of financing, and hosting many foreign guests of means and repute. But on it did go.

Back-to-back snowfalls in such amounts following recent years of minimal snow and warm winters apparently caught village administration off guard, actually asleep. Then one day the bear awoke. Heavy-duty frontend loaders and large dump trucks invaded the normally carless, quiet Bahnhofstrasse and finally got the job done.

Unlike what one might expect in the USA (see Chicago, defeat of Mayor Bilandic by storm), the Swiss local populace were loathe to criticize. All excuses are found to remain passive and polite. There might have been muttering in private, but no public denunciation of the incompetence.

The following response by the Swiss was typical: "We have to remember that we are in the mountains here."

Well, all of Switzerland you might say is, more or less, in the mountains. And whether an elderly person winds up in the hospital with a broken hip walking on the main street of Zurich or Zermatt makes little difference. But criticism of the powers that be, even when they clearly deserve it, comes only with difficulty here. Nevertheless, someone seems to have gotten the message. The winter season of 2019 saw much improved snow removal and a welcome new emphasis on cleaning sidewalks.

That snowfall also took its toll on local infrastructure. For example, the aerial tramway to the Rothorn mountain peak and restaurant, a popular destination and a paragliding jump-off point, had to be closed down for months. One of the supporting masts for the cable car had shifted out of place, thereby creating a risk to passengers. Not to worry too much; the area is loaded with plenty of other ways to get to the tops of peaks.

***

When weather turns bleak, mountains become confining, leading to brooding and melancholy. You can suffocate in fog and the absence of even a short horizon here. After three years, I sensed that life without the welcome intrusion of interesting guests from all parts of the world could well turn to boredom in tiny Zermatt.

I had no family here. Entering the inner circle of the Swiss was like trying to drill into a bank vault during business hours. And to find what?

I had lived or worked in New Zealand, Zimbabwe, South Africa and Canada. Nowhere did I have such difficulties finding easygoing, pleasant, simple relationships with the locals who were not foreigners.

I have referred to Zermatt as a relatively isolated village. The key word is "relatively." In fact, nothing in Switzerland is isolated as such. Getting lost without the previous consumption of large quantities of alcohol is impossible.

Even in Zermatt's mountainous surroundings, you are likely to be rescued quickly by helicopter or otherwise, as the area is flooded with alpinists and hikers. So I was amused to hear the story of a panicked American tech writer who, on arrival as my guest, breathlessly explained that his vehicle's GPS had conked out on one of the mountain passes.

"I almost didn't make it here," he exclaimed.

Incredulous, I could not help myself: "Have you heard of something called a folding map?"

In fact, even a road map may be unnecessary in Switzerland. Virtually every main highway is well marked with a sign indicating distances and, for hiking paths, also the time to the destination. Wilderness in any true sense is unknown.

Next morning, with my guest's new phone still causing him trouble, he proclaimed that he might not be able to drive to Germany as he had intended. Eventually his phone problems were solved and he was able to depart, but the dependence on technology in doing what everyone had routinely done without the internet until just a few years ago was remarkable.

Across the board, my guests are all more or less dependent on their smartphones, as one would expect. Some more so than others. As I have no desire to be a martinet, I do not prevent guests from using their phones as we eat together, something that I personally eschew. In fact, one young Korean man had his mother instructing him, from South Korea, on what to eat as we were eating!

For me, without guests arriving from all over the world, Zermatt would by now have settled into the routine and mundane. There just might not be enough variation. But alas, I can still transit elsewhere vicariously, through my guests.

One day I can have as a guest a tall, muscle-defined, testosterone-saturated U.S. Marine guard visiting on his holiday from work at the United States Embassy in Sweden. He, when offered a cup of tea on arrival, pulled a quart of Jim Beam from his duffel bag, put on an unmistakable frown and objected: "I don't drink tea."

And it got worse. My Marine asked about the association between my "Eagle's Nest" location description and the original Eagle's Nest. I was taken aback at first, not realizing that anyone would confuse my location name with a Clint Eastwood thriller or the German Obersalzberg mountain retreat near the Bavarian town of Berchtesgaden. That site had been used exclusively during World War II by members of the Nazi Party and was, on occasion, haunted by Hitler himself. When I informed him that there was no connection, and he found no Nazi memorabilia scattered in the apartment, he was clearly disappointed.

"There are two world leaders that I respect," he informed me. "Vladimir Putin first, and Donald Trump."

"Oh, yeah?" I remarked casually, trying to concentrate on an NPR program on racism in the South that I was listening to as he pontificated.

"And listening to NPR won't get you any real news, either, you know," he scolded.

If I had the slightest suspicion that the name "Eagle's Nest" would attract neo-Nazi crazies to Zermatt, I would instantly change the name to something like "The Sparrow's Hideout." But I have no fear that the Marine will recommend me to his fellow white supremacists. Not long after he left I read that the Marines had ousted a number of their members for being white supremacists.

In the very next week I was able to greet a more pleasant, garrulous, German Army lieutenant who lectured me, stating in all seriousness that Germany and Russia should team up together in a natural type of arrangement, ensuring Germany the raw materials that it needs as an economic power. I wanted to remind him: been there, done that, but I listened without comment. He went on more spectacularly:

"The German soldier, unlike soldiers of other armies, has a tradition of thinking for himself, acting on his own," he explained.

"Wow," I thought. This was a revelation. Suddenly I felt as if I were a character in an altered version of *A Christmas Carol.* The ghost of John Wayne appeared before me, and intoned, "Now look here, pilgrim, I spent my time fighting the Japs in the Pacific, but I have Army buddies who fought in Europe, and that just ain't so."

The Duke may have had Army buddies, but certainly not from shared combat. He never spent a day in military service; he was too busy making movies for director John Ford. But anyway, he was absolutely right about this. It was revisionist history of the worst kind.

The default mode for any belief system over time is always the story that leans to one's own good, whether a Nazi past or a Confederate past or any other. No one wants to think they're bad. So history just gets revised. It's the same with any story. The truth has to fit what you can bear.

And where would I be today without the ever-persistent advice (for four days, mind you) from an American man who had just taken one of those courses on how to seduce women. The internet ads at issue promise instruction on how to take advantage of a "loophole" in the female mind.

"Women love puppies," he instructed. "If you get a puppy, they'll hover around you. Then you can make your move. But you have to show them that you can take care of something that is alive, even plants in the home will do the trick."

"Show who," I asked. "The puppies?"

I like puppies, but I don't have a puppy. I do have houseplants, thank God, so I felt adequately prepared for seduction should the need arise.

And not to forget the Korean woman who failed to understand the purpose of a shower curtain, flooded the bathroom floor but good, and then asked me, "Where is the floor drain?"

Apparently, I discovered, Koreans have bathrooms meant to flood, complete with floor drains and no bathroom rugs. Lesson learned on my part. The guest was so sincere and sorrowful that I instantly forgave her, but thereafter never forgot to instruct Korean guests on the use of a shower curtain.

Then we had the twenty-year-old genius (literally) from a farm near Shanghai. The government of China had paid for her education at a renowned school of economics in the Swiss city of St. Gallen. Within minutes of her arrival, she was sketching faithful reproductions of artwork that hung on my wall with her pencil. But there was a twist; she explained how she instantly recognizes what she called the center point of any painting, a point from which the painting radiates into its peripheral parts, a concept that I had never even heard of.

To prove this, she began to figuratively pull apart my artwork, disassembling it into constitutive parts that she then drew for me while she explained what she was doing. (I'm still not sure. Later, however, I discovered that the American abstract expressionist painter, Jackson Pollock, also spoke of his paintings as radiating from a central point.)

I have kept her pencil drawings to this day. Before she left to go back home to China, she overwhelmed me with the drawing that now graces the cover of this book, framed in black on my wall. Such endearing acts will remain with me forever, enriching me, the result of opening my home to total strangers.

But then again, there was the eighty-year-old Chinese man who visited and explained merrily that he was finally traveling the world... without his wife. On the first morning of his stay, in the darkness of about 5 a.m., I heard rustling and bubbling noises emerge from his area. When I got up to look, he was boiling eggs in an electric pot on his desk, and preparing some other concoction. I explained carefully that the kitchen would be the proper place for such activity, and at about 7:30 a.m. as well. Oh, he laughed his wonderful, toothy laugh, and went right on cooking his eggs.

Had this been some younger guy, the show would have been over. But this clever fox knew just how to manipulate me with distracting stories and plenty of laughter. I tried again: cooking in the kitchen only, I instructed, and with my coordination. Hah hah, oh that was funny, apparently. Every time I turned my back, eggs were boiling in his pot.

Well, overall he more or less won. But I did prevail when he tried a bridge too far and moved his boiling pot to the living area.

"Would you like sleeping in the cold?" I asked.

Oh, that was another cue for laughter, but I think he realized I meant it. The limit was finally set. By the time he left, I felt great fondness for this courageous, elderly man.

Just as I instruct my guests on where to go and what to see in Zermatt, they have lessons for me as well, inadvertent though some may be … like the Chinese man who stayed with me for only one day.

XVI.　The Binoculars

"We shall not cease from exploration, and the end of all our exploring will be to arrive where we started and know the place for the first time."
~ T.S. Elliott, American poet and essayist

I don't remember how they came into my possession. As I thought about that, the best answer that I could think of was that they had belonged to the departed husband of an old friend in Interlaken. He was a bird watcher. One day, while cleaning out some drawers, she must have come across them and offered them to me as a gift. This made sense, but I cannot honestly say that I remember the particular transfer clearly.

I would never have contemplated any of this history had I not had a careless Chinese guest visit me. As I had done countless times with other guests, I offered him the binoculars for his excursion into the mountains. I hardly ever used them personally. I failed to consider their existence, except for those times of sharing. They just sat there, on the glass table, in their cheap, imitation leather case. Surely I would have gone to my grave oblivious of their significance, except for one thing: my Chinese guest returned and jolted me into binocular awareness by flatly admitting, "I'm sorry, I lost your binoculars. I must have left them on the train."

His pronouncement put me into a state of confusion. The binoculars had been a part of my household for years. On the one hand, I had hardly ever used them personally, so it could be said they had little personal value. On the other hand, I derived pleasure from lending them out. Now they were gone.

Without my saying a word, my guest said, "I want to pay for them, what were they worth?" Far too quickly I ventured a pure but uneducated guess and said, "Oh, I suppose they would cost about fifty francs or so." My guest, an honorable fellow, reached into his wallet and insisted I erase his debt.

"Thank you," I replied, "I will replace them for use by other guests."

After he left, I considered the money he had given me. Then, quite irrationally and unpredictably, those binoculars began to occupy my thoughts as never before. The loss annoyed me. Obsession would be only a minor overstatement. *Why hadn't I used them more often, or at all?* I asked myself.

I peered around outside, down into the valley below. Why hadn't I explored using the binoculars? Why hadn't I examined the waterfall across the valley more closely? Or the hotels, nearby? Suddenly, a multitude of lost opportunities assaulted me. What then motivated me to replace the binoculars wasn't just to be able to lend them to future guests, but to use them to accomplish what I had never valued about them before. I was, not exaggeratedly, emotionally driven to replace them.

I checked the internet. To my surprise I realized that I had been conservative in my appraisal of their value, by far. But I also considered that I would have felt uncomfortable charging my guest 150 or 200 francs or more. I informed a friend, Bruno the chief paragliding pilot, about my error. Some hours later he phoned and said, "I have a replacement pair for you. I found a special deal, and you won't believe the price: exactly fifty francs, plus postage."

And so misfortune turned around with some luck. To my surprise again, the new pair was as good as the original, or possible better. I used the new pair to accomplish everything I had ignored with the old pair: waterfall gazing, train station examination, mountaintops, paragliders in flight. I even used them at night, partially in the hope—pushed aside from immediate consciousness or admission—of perhaps spying some young lady in a state of semi-undress before she closed the curtains. No such luck.

The new pair of binoculars received good, intense use … for just about two weeks. Currently, they sit on a credenza, again almost never used or thought of. But there has been a change in my attitude towards them. I check for their presence from time to time, for some sort of reassurance. I recall the feeling of loss. On the occasions when I do use them, the motivation to do so seems to come more from the memory of the loss of the first pair, the old pair, the unappreciated pair, rather than from the excitement of what I might see by using them. And this, I consider, is an important lesson in life taught to me by a careless guest.

An understanding that valuing what I have in the first place is not an innate feature of my mind. The lesson needs to be learned. And it is easily forgotten, to be relearned, over and over, right up to the end presumably. If you can't lose something, it may never come to have any value.

The binoculars unexpectedly became a metaphor for my life, as I look back now with greater awareness. Losses always blindsided me, and even when I did occasionally dread them as if to forestall them, they arrived on their own schedule anyway. Once at hand, those losses did not replace themselves like my binoculars. Painful work needed to be done to overcome each one, to have me emerge on a higher level from which to gaze at the landscape.

***

Some months ago, with Scandinavian and California wildfires prominent in the news along with record high European temperatures and severe drought, I headed to the *Kirchbrücke,* binoculars in hand. I gazed once more at the timeless Matterhorn. As usual, the spot was packed with visitors taking pictures. What struck me, however, was the torrent of water flowing down the Vispa River, right below me under the bridge. I studied the sky around the Matterhorn; there had been no rain in the mountains. That would be the usual explanation for the high volume of water. Boulders typically protrude above a modestly flowing stream on blue-sky days. Not so now, nothing but roiling, angry grey swirls and spouts catapulting over submerged rocks. This was mountain treasure flowing past us in frighteningly impressive volumes.

The view from the bridge reminded me of a watercolor I had seen of the village at a friend's house, depicting it as it appeared about one hundred and fifty years ago. To my surprise it showed the Gorner Glacier descend practically all the way to the level of the village. Today, it is nowhere near being in sight of the village, and losing mass rapidly far above.

Swiss glaciers are melting quicker than most others and have been retreating steadily since 2001. As glaciers retreat, entirely new valleys emerge. Some of these valleys will lend themselves to the construction of new dams and power production in the future. But the end game is clear. In 2018 alone, Swiss glaciers lost an average of two and a half percent of their mass, and the loss would have been worse had it not been for an extraordinarily snowy winter.

There was a time when Nature dominated the Swiss, as it did all of mankind. Over time we found we had the power to make that seem otherwise. Or at least so it was thought for a time. As it turns out, you can alter every meandering stream in Switzerland and make it flow straight, gaining precious land for the effort. But suddenly you find, for example, that fish no longer reproduce because you have changed spawning grounds and water temperatures.

The thing about living in the midst of Nature, as opposed to a city, is that it causes a reflection on time itself. Compared to a city, so many things around us here in Zermatt are timeless. Yet things do change, and for a reason.

I am a bit jealous perhaps, considering that Lady Matterhorn doesn't change while I age. She doesn't care about me, while I contemplate her often. Each time that I see her I stop, in mind or body, reflecting on the astounding beauty that she hosts. She has had many suitors and will have many more, without aging at all herself. But then again, the current times are telling us that things can change, even for what seems like timeless Nature, and far faster than we can imagine.

With coral reefs around the world collapsing and insect populations from Europe to South America down by an astounding seventy-five to eighty percent, there is a message that needs to be heard.

Drought, a circumstance unheard of here and considered near impossible for what the Swiss know is an often and reliably rain-soaked, cool-temperature landscape, suddenly spread ominously throughout the country in 2018. Aside from the need for water in agriculture, hydroelectric power—the most efficient source of electrical power by far—supplies a large portion (60%) of Swiss power needs from mountain dams. Those dams need water that will run out.

Everyone knows, or should know, that the villain is carbon dioxide. But the very cure for our glacier melt in the future might also include, in the extreme, the end of Zermatt as a travel destination, among many other destinations of course. Most people require large quantities of jet fuel to get here. My guests, who bring me such pleasure and lead to fond memories, are not local. They are one part of the problem and thus my having them as visitors is also unavoidably a part of the problem.

Climate change has come to reflect my interest in the topic of fake news, combined with science. Too many of us have been misled intentionally on the subject of a warming Earth by people who knew better. It should make us angry.

I feel so strongly about climate change, habitat destruction and the dangers to the web of life that they pose, that I often discuss these topics with my guests, especially the state of the oceans. The lack of knowledge is distressingly ubiquitous and profound, but I have also found that facts do raise awareness, at least with some of my younger visitors.

To demonstrate the difference between common, incorrect perception and reality, I start off, for example, by asking guests the following question: Which contains more mass, the oceans or the atmosphere? By far, most people answer incorrectly, including even a cloud scientist who visited me from the National Oceanic and Atmospheric Administration (NOAA) in Boulder,

Colorado. Eighty percent of guests respond that the atmosphere has more mass. The correct answer is the opposite to the extreme: The oceans contain from five-hundred to one-thousand times as much mass as the atmosphere.

What is the point? The atmosphere may well be vast in volume, which presumably influences the incorrect answer, but in fact there isn't much there. This should lead to a consideration of the fact that, if there isn't much there, the proportions of what *is* there can be influenced relatively easily. The oceans have already been seriously polluted. Just what and how much carbon dioxide can we continue to jam into the atmosphere and expect that there will be … constancy as we like it? It doesn't stand to reason. And it is instructive to consider that, if carbon dioxide were not invisible, it would have been tamed long ago.

As fossil fuel companies and right-wing politics have captured the belief systems of too many Americans regarding man's contribution to global temperature rise, I ask a second, different question to bring home the point that carbon emissions are harmful from another perspective. Here, the evidence is immediately demonstrable and convincing. I ask: If we assume for a moment that man is not contributing significantly to increased global temperatures, would there be any other reason to stop emitting carbon into the atmosphere through the burning of fossil fuels?

On this question I get puzzled looks. I then explain that one-third of every tank of gasoline burned, for example, winds up in the oceans. There, undeniably, the carbon dioxide from the combustion makes the water more acidic. This is not theory; anyone can take a pH reading (measure of acidity) in a glass of tap water, using litmus paper. Comparing the readings after blowing exhaled air from the lungs into the water with a soda straw will show a shift to the more acidic.

As oceans become more acidic, shellfish in particular can no longer develop normally and reef ecosystems also die off. As of today, reef ocean ecosystems appear to have little chance of surviving our carbon onslaught. They, in turn, are home to about one-third of all fish at some time in their lifecycles.

There is another aspect to the second question that I pose. It has emerged that providing carbon dioxide to the air through the burning of fossil fuels has not turned into the beneficial "fertilizer" that the fossil-fuel folks once misleadingly promised in television advertisements that hoodwinked the American public. This was another, deliberate fake news story. Instead of fertilizing, it has been shown by direct measurement that plants, for example rice—one of the world's most important sources of nutrition—have a lower protein-to-carbohydrate ratio in an atmosphere higher in carbon. Protein, the nutrient most expensive and most lacking in the diets of much of the world's population, diminishes in proportion to increased carbohydrate formation.

While man's contribution to global warming may remain as unsettled for some as knowing whose religion is right, these two other detrimental effects of carbon are immediately knowable. If they are not accepted then it is a further display of the irrationality of a propagandized American population, those who feel safer having others do their thinking for them.

As I thought more about the problem of wholesale denial of impending environmental doom (Yes, doom; you cannot eliminate eighty percent of insect life, the bottom of the food chain, for example, and not expect doom.), I realized that we have experienced similar, mass-denial phenomena in other regards. Recall the collective denial of the housing boom and its bust in 2008. Well, that obviously couldn't happen, until it did. The reason it couldn't happen? Because it was unthinkable; too many people would be affected, too many lives changed. This reasoning is not adequate for our future survival. In finance and economics, you can gain an edge on others by "shorting" an existing situation that is ripe for implosion. We cannot "short" the environment.

***

I have spent considerable effort in this book on aspects of my personal history and how beliefs that are easy but false have impacted my life. There is nothing more important to the survival of—without exaggeration—our entire species on Planet Earth, however, than understanding how intentionally planted, false beliefs about the nature of Nature are harming us. I therefore hope for a merged impact on the reader deriving from this book: a contemplation of what we believe to be true from a bit of my history, mixed-in with understanding that penetrating any smoke screen of fake news …. could also actually help save the world!

In final reflection on my hosting, I have asked myself how I might have reacted years ago if someone had suggested the idea of starting an Airbnb-type business. I suspect I would not have agreed that it could work out well. Letting strangers into your home? Oh, come on! Infinite problems ahead. But clearly not so, as I have asked every guest about their experiences with other Airbnbs and have seldom heard complaints. The concept is overwhelmingly popular. That suggests that maybe we overestimate our own sanctity and underestimate the goodness in others.

So many of my guests are searchers in their travels. In their seeking, they have rewarded me with joyous experiences, happy memories and lessons that I could never have imagined learning without their visits. I intend to continue with my hosting as I have, because this lifestyle provides not only entertainment, but the growth of my soul.

Zermatt is a good place to live and to visit. It has been good to me and good for me. I look forward to my next guest ... a Canadian from Calgary.

Epilogue

So it is that I have now exhausted my reservoir of subject matter that I thought would be of interest to a reader. Having arrived at my goals and the end of this book, just like any reader who faces an ending, I now ask: What's next?

Endings are difficult. The problem with them is that we do not see endings for what they mask: new beginnings. Seeing endings as preludes to beginnings is so important that every child should learn how to handle endings in grade school. At some junction in life the concept may come to mean more to survival than reading, writing or arithmetic.

As alluded to earlier in this book, I arrived in Zermatt following the death of a friend and after my career as a scientist and editor at a Swiss university was terminated. That ending was the result of misinformation piped into the internet with great effort and swallowed whole by a Swiss university— a poor showing indeed.

The effort, to promote a false history about me, was fueled by lawyers in Milwaukee, Wisconsin. Their motivation, it is safe to assume, was and still is payment toward the more than one million dollars that I owe them due to a defamation lawsuit; the legal system in Milwaukee saw fit to rename truthful information on lawyer corruption there—as detailed in the book *Beyond Outrage*—calling it defamation.

But as one story ends another begins, and right from here in Zermatt, even as I continue to welcome guests from all over the world. I have my new work cut out for me.

In earlier books and here, I described injustice in the American legal system in its rudiment as the modification of true stories into false but official stories. That transformation is facilitated by the concealment of evidence and the induction of fear. A culture apart, in Switzerland, I have found the same tactics employed by Swiss lawyers. And why not? Lawyer motivation in Switzerland is the same as in the USA: survival within their system.

In the criminal justice system of both countries, a defendant is like a mirage, shimmering with reward but quick to disappear. What always remains is the system, the established power centers, the lawyers with more influential carriers who determine whether a young, idealistic lawyer can earn a living after his scholarly investment. So at the end to this book I have come full circle; I left the USA to continue writing stories about corruption in the American legal system. Now, I have another story to tell, about corruption in another legal system, this time the Swiss.

As thankful as I am that I have been permitted to continue writing the truth in the country of my birth, I see that Swiss lawyers also wish to conceal the true story of my time at a Swiss university and my true history, oddly precipitated by influence from Milwaukee.

I thus bid farewell to my readers from one, hopefully entertaining and intellectually rewarding adventure, to next provide another, darker and more sinister exposé of the mechanisms of legal system dysfunction in the Alpine Democracy.

About the Author

The author has lived in Switzerland for over 15 years, experiencing the perspectives of both the native insider to Switzerland and the foreigner. He has hosted over 500 guests in Zermatt to date, consistently reaching Airbnb Superhost status.

Trained in biology and the biomedical sciences, he has taught at the University of Wisconsin and the University of Basel. Today he translates science texts and edits science research papers, especially relating to neurosurgery. He has also been active for over 20 years in exposing legal system corruption, both in Switzerland and the USA. This, in turn, has provoked false, vicious internet attacks in the form of fake news.

Two previous books, *Beyond Outrage* (www.beyond-outrage.com) and *Lawyers Broken Bad* (www.lawyersbrokenbad.com) expound in detail on legal mechanisms of injustice, with explanatory models.

Bibliography

Kandel, Eric R., (2006). *In Search of Memory*. W. W. Norton & Company, Inc., New York, NY, USA.

Dawkins, Richard, (2004). *The Ancestor's Tale*. Weidenfeld & Nicolson, Orion Publishing Group, London, U.K.

Kahneman, Daniel, (2011). *Thinking Fast and Slow*. Penguin Group Publishers, London, England.

Hawkins, Jeff, (2004). *On Intelligence*. Times Books, New York, NY, USA.

Wallace-Wells, David, (2019). *The Uninhabitable Earth; A Story of the Future*. Penguin Random House Publishers, London, U.K.

Martel, Frédéric, (2019). *In the Closet of the Vatican: Power, Homosexuality, Hypocrisy*. Bloomsbury Publishing, London, U.K

Inglin, Mark, (2018). *Lawyers Broken Bad*. Available on Amazon: www.lawyersbrokenbad.com.